Teaching
for
Competence

Teaching for Competence

HOWARD SULLIVAN
NORMAN HIGGINS
College of Education
Arizona State University

Teachers College, Columbia University
New York and London   1983

Published by Teachers College Press, 1234 Amsterdam Avenue, New York, N.Y. 10027

Library of Congress Cataloging in Publication Data

Sullivan, Howard J.
  Teaching for competence.

  Includes index.
  1. Teaching—Handbooks, manuals, etc.   2. Teachers—
attitudes. I. Higgins, Norman. II. Title.
LB1025.2.S923 1983   371.1'02   82-19584

ISBN 0-8077-2725-3

Manufactured in the United States of America

88 87 86 85 84   2 3 4 5 6

CONTENTS

PREFACE

The basic content for *Teaching for Competence* resulted from a systematic course-development effort at Arizona State University (ASU) and a succession of tryouts that extended over a three-year period. Ten instructors and more than 400 preservice and inservice teachers participated in the tryouts. The materials were regularly revised during this period on the basis of achievement and attitude data collected during the tryouts.

The final tryout was conducted during a single semester with five classes of preservice and inservice teachers enrolled at ASU. Each class was taught by a different instructor. A separate 40-item pretest for each chapter was administered prior to the instruction on what now constitutes Chapters 2, 3, and 4. A 40-item posttest for each chapter was administered following the instruction for the chapter.

Average pretest and posttest percentage scores on each of the three 40-item tests are shown below.

Chapter	Test	Pretest Average	Posttest Average
2	Worthwhile Objectives	59%	88%
3	Effective Instruction	49%	90%
4	Assessment	64%	89%
	Average	57%	89%

As shown, pretest scores on the three tests ranged from 49 to 64 percent and averaged 57 percent. Posttest scores ranged from 88 to 90 percent and averaged 89 percent.

Students in the final tryout also completed an attitude questionnaire on which they indicated their degree of agreement (agree, neutral, disagree) with four evaluation statements about the course. Attitudes were very favorable. The majority of students agreed that the course content was relevant (87%), the course was well taught (89%), they learned a lot (78%), and it was a good course (82%). The highest number of students indicating disagreement with any statement was 8 percent.

The authors wish to express their appreciation to the many individuals who contributed to the preparation of this book. These include Dr. Muriel Bebeau, Barbara Mead, Elizabeth Outcalt, Dr. Robert Reiser, and the instructors and students who participated in the book's development and field testing. The contributions of Judy Larson, who suggested the ideas for illustrations, and of Robert B. Martin, who drew the illustrations, are also gratefully acknowledged.

Chapter 1

A MATTER OF ACCOMPLISHMENT

When Lucy of the "Peanuts" comic strip said that she was thinking of starting something new, Charlie Brown replied that it was a good idea because the people who get the most out of life are those who try to accomplish something. "Accomplish something?" exclaimed Lucy. "I thought we were just supposed to keep busy!"

Accomplishing something is what this book is about. It presents a straightforward, effective method for good teaching. We have chosen to call the book *Teaching for Competence*. There were several reasons for picking this title. First, the teaching approach described in the book has become known as competency-based instruction, or just CBI, because it is based on the idea of teaching specific skills or competencies. Second, we believe that teachers who use this method will become more competent teachers, even though they may already be very good. Third, we also believe that students who are taught by this approach will become more competent at what they are taught. Thus, the CBI method enables both teachers and students to accomplish something—the something that is the very essence of their roles as teachers and learners.

TEACHING STUDENTS TO DO SOMETHING

We see CBI both as a way of thinking about instruction and as a way of instructing. Though each of us believes strongly in it, we don't always agree on every CBI issue. When we decided to write this book, one of us (Sullivan) said to the other, "Higgins, I'd be happy if the people who use the book just learn to *think about* instruction in the CBI way."

"That's all? Just think about it that way?" protested Higgins. "I also want them to *do* it that way."

"That's asking a lot," replied Sullivan, "but let's give it a try. I'll gladly settle for either one."

Our purpose in recreating our conversation here is not, as you might suspect, so that you will learn our names. It's to illustrate an important principle. *Good instruction teaches students to do something.* Sullivan would be happy, though not completely ecstatic, if after finishing this book you consistently think in the CBI manner about your instruction. Higgins, on the other hand, would like more than that. He wants you to actually do your instruction—to plan and present it—CBI style. The point is that in both cases the authors want you to *do something*: either to think a certain way about instruction or to do it that way. This point may seem trivial to you. It's not. Don't just think of the act of teaching as presenting information. Think of it as teaching your students to do something. You'll be more effective if you think that way.

WHY CBI?

Competency-based instruction, as you may know, is a rather controversial topic among educators. Although CBI enjoys considerable popularity, not everyone is on the bandwagon by any means. There are arguments on both sides of the issue. We want to give you some reasons for learning about CBI because we believe that if you have to learn something, there should be a good reason for doing it. Then we'll turn to some of the arguments against CBI.

The best reason for learning the CBI approach, in our opinion, is that it is an effective teaching method. You want your students to learn the most important content for your grade or subject areas, and you want to teach it well. That is precisely the focus of CBI.

A second reason is that you may work as a teacher, either now or later, in a competency-oriented school program. Competency programs, not all of them good, are becoming widespread. Well over half the states have taken action, through their legislatures or state boards of education, to require some form of competency program in the schools. Your state may well be one of them. Many school districts have taken similar steps. Learning the CBI method will enable you to understand the basic elements of a good competency-based program and to work well within one.

Still a third reason for learning about CBI is for your own professional

knowledge as an informed educator. The objectives-instruction-assessment approach to teaching that characterizes CBI is very popular in the field of education today. Every teacher should be familiar with it, as well as with other teaching methods, whether or not he or she chooses to use it.

AND WHY NOT?

Now let's consider some arguments on the other side of the issue. We have selected what are perhaps the four major objections that opponents of CBI raise against it. Naturally, we think some of these arguments are pretty bad. When we think that, we tell you. We also encourage you to explore these issues further on your own or with others.

1. *Competency-based instruction is a dehumanizing or dispassionate process.* Some CBI opponents argue that CBI focuses more on the

competencies to be learned than on the individual learner. They contend that it therefore is not a humane method. Now that simply isn't true. Any sensible teaching process must take into account both the learners and what they are to be taught. CBI is heavily learner-oriented because the whole approach is organized around helping students learn what is worthwhile for them. The individual learners are the most important element. The competencies and the method are important too.

In and of itself, CBI has nothing to do with humaneness or passion. Neither do other teaching methods. CBI is simply a way to teach effectively. It is the teacher, not the teaching method, who is or is not humane to students. As advocates of CBI, we believe that you should always treat your students with respect, enthusiasm, kindness, and understanding. We teach CBI style in our own classes, and we like to think of ourselves as being nice people. You too can use CBI while retaining your own special orientation to students. Will the teaching method you choose really make you a more or less humane person? Do nicer people choose one particular method? Of course not.

2. *CBI stifles teacher creativity.* This is another weak argument, but stick with us. The last two are better.

The point that CBI opponents make on this issue is that the advance planning you do in CBI limits your options to be creative during instruction or to take advantage of unanticipated teaching opportunities that arise. Somehow, deciding in advance what students should learn, how to teach it, and how to check on whether they learned it are seen as "locking you in" to a fixed routine of instruction. Now, that's incredible! It's much like saying that, after leaving on a preplanned drive from your home to some other place, you can't change your mind about where you are going or the route you will take to get there.

Be creative in your teaching, both when planning it and when opportunities arise during instruction. At the same time, be sure that your creativity has a good instructional purpose: either improved student learning or greater enjoyment during the learning process. Creativity is compatible with CBI and with any other reasonable teaching method. It's also desirable.

3. *Important learnings may be underemphasized compared with less important ones.* This is a crucial matter to consider in all teaching methods. No matter what method you use, it's easy to lose sight of what's most important for students to learn. Students should be taught the big skills and ideas essential to their intellectual and social well-

being. Sometimes smaller skills are so much more apparent and easier to teach that we may forget about the bigger picture. Yet, big skills and ideas must be built upon a solid foundation of smaller ones. Both are necessary.

One of the key elements of CBI is deciding what your students should learn. When you do this, keep a firm eye on the skills and attitudes that are most important. That will help you strike a good balance in your teaching between these major, comprehensive skills and the smaller foundational skills on which they are built.

You will note later that part of Chapter 2 deals with how to identify skills and attitudes that are most worthwhile for students to learn.

4. *We don't know how to set good standards for competency testing programs.* This point we agree with. It's a valid criticism of minimum competency testing programs but not of competency-based instruction. Don't confuse the two. The word "competency" is the same but the ideas are vastly different. Minimum competency testing programs have typically been established by state legislatures, not by educators, on a statewide basis. They now exist in many states. These programs normally require that students attain a certain standard on a statewide test in order to progress beyond their current level—for example, to graduate from high school or to pass beyond the eighth grade or other grade levels.

There are serious problems with minimum competency testing programs in some states. One is that there often has been little or no effort to make sure that what is tested is what has been taught in the schools. Another is that we do not know what is a good minimum "pass" score (or standard) to set, particularly before the test has been widely administered. If minimum standards are set without this knowledge, as they have been in the first year of competency testing programs in some states, excessive numbers of students may fail the test and suffer serious consequences.

Testing in the schools should be closely tied to the instructional program. That is a basic feature of CBI and a basic problem with many minimum competency testing programs. Further, standards for minimum test scores, if set at all, should be established only after data are available to indicate how well students can be expected to score on the test.

CBI AND THIS BOOK

What does CBI mean to you as a teacher? Basically there are three things.

- You decide what your students should learn.
- You teach it well.
- You check to see if the students have learned it.

This book is organized around these three topics. Chapter 2, Worthwhile Objectives, deals with deciding what content your students should learn. Chapter 3, Effective Instruction, covers teaching it well. Chapter 4, Assessment, describes checking to see how well the students have learned what you taught. A final chapter, Making CBI Work, explains how to put the whole system of objectives-instruction-assessment together so that it really works.

Chapters 2 through 4, then, cover the basic elements of CBI. Early in each of these chapters you will find a list of the skills you should learn from the chapter. The remainder of the chapter consists of information and short exercises to help you learn these skills. At the end of the chapter you will be referred to a self test that will enable you to tell how well you have done.

Included at the end of all five chapters are suggestions for additional learning activities. You may use these activities to extend your knowledge about the topics covered and to apply this knowledge to various educational situations. Many of the additional learning activities are well suited for cooperative work by small or large groups.

Here are the procedures we recommend that you use as you read each chapter.

- Read attentively.
- Complete each exercise in the chapter without looking back in the text or ahead at the answers.
- After completing an exercise, check your answers against those given in the text.
- After you finish the chapter, take the self test over it.

Good luck on the exercises and self tests. We hope you like the book.

ADDITIONAL LEARNING ACTIVITIES

1. Locate, read, and discuss in class one or more articles that deal with the pros and cons of competency-based instruction. One brief debate-type article that we recommend is given here.

    Larson, J., and Weninger, A. English Programs Should Be Competency Based: Pro and Con. *English Journal*, November, 1980, *69*, pages 8–12.

2. Read and discuss in class articles dealing with minimum competency testing programs. We suggest that different individuals read each of the four articles listed here. Collectively these works describe the various types of state competency testing programs, issues related to minimal competency testing, and the early problems with a program in one state. All four articles are from the same issue of *Phi Delta Kappan*, May, 1978, *50*.

    Pipho, C. Minimum Competency Testing in 1978: A Look at State Standards, pages 585–589.

    Brickell, H. Seven Key Notes on Minimal Competency Testing, pages 589–592.

    Glass, G. Minimum Competence and Incompetence in Florida, pages 602–605.

    Fremer, J. In Response to Gene Glass, pages 605–606.

3. If you don't already know this, check to see whether your state has a minimum competency testing program or any other type of competency-oriented program. If so, learn what you can about the program from the State Department of Education or another appropriate agency. For example, for a minimum competency

testing program, try to get at least the following information.

a. At what grade levels and with what subjects does it operate?

b. How does it work—that is, what are the procedures involved?

c. What percentage of students passed and what percentage failed last year? What were the consequences for those who failed?

d. What changes, if any, are being planned in the program? Why?

If your state or a school district in your area has a competency-oriented program, talk with administrators and/or teachers to get their reactions to it. Discuss the information you obtain and the pros and cons of the programs with others.

Chapter 2

WORTHWHILE OBJECTIVES

As you now know, deciding what your students should learn is the first major step in competency-based instruction. Many sources are available to help you with this task: textbooks, curriculum guides, other teachers, your own training and experience, and perhaps your students on some occasions. Your goal here is to come up with the skills and attitudes that you want your students to acquire. These skills and attitudes are often called "instructional objectives." That's the name that we'll use throughout this book, although the term "competencies" is also used commonly in CBI as a synonym for "instructional objectives."

Good instructional objectives are the foundation for CBI. As the teacher, you use them as the basis for planning your instruction and for assessing student learning. The use of instructional objectives to indicate what students should learn is now commonplace in the schools. Teachers in many districts are expected or required to write objectives for their courses.

This chapter teaches you to write good instructional objectives. Upon completing it, you should be able to:

- Distinguish between instructional objectives and instructional activities
- Identify worthwhile instructional objectives
- Identify well-written instructional objectives
- Write instructional objectives

These four skills, as you may have guessed, are our own instructional objectives for this chapter, written in abridged form. That is, they are what we think you should learn from the chapter. The instruction and self test that follow are based closely on these objectives. Together the objectives, instruction, and assessment (the self test) are the basic elements of the competency-based instruction method that is used in this chapter and in Chapters 3 and 4.

DISTINGUISHING OBJECTIVES FROM ACTIVITIES

A common error in working with instructional objectives is to confuse objectives and activities. Objectives represent ends of instruction; activities represent means to these ends. *An objective describes a skill or attitude that students will be expected to possess after instruction.* In contrast, *an activity is a learning experience in which students participate for the purpose of attaining an objective.* The distinction between an activity and an objective is illustrated by the following statements.

1. The student will view a filmstrip about famous Indian legends and their significance in an Indian culture.
2. The student will tell at least three well-known Indian legends and describe the significance of each in an Indian culture.

You can see that the first statement is an example of an activity. It is an experience in which students might participate for the purpose of learning about Indian legends. The second statement, on the other hand, is an instructional objective—a skill that the teacher might want students to acquire from a unit on Indians.

Exercise 2.1 provides practice in distinguishing between instructional objectives and instructional activities. Answer all of the items. Then check your answers against those directly following the exercise. After you have finished, go on to exercise 2.2.

EXERCISE 2.1. Distinguishing Objectives from Activities

Write an O in the blank beside each instructional objective and an A beside each instructional activity. If you think that an item could be both an objective and an activity, mark it as an objective.

a. _____ The student will solve long-division problems.

b. _____ The student will sound out and read new words.

c. _____ The student will practice multiplication tables.

d. _____ The student will take a field trip to the art museum.

e. _____ The student will name four Shakespearean plays and write a brief plot summary of each.

Items a, b, and e are objectives. Each describes a skill that teachers might want students to possess after instruction in particular subject areas. Items c and d are activities—experiences in which students could participate for learning purposes.

EXERCISE 2.2. Distinguishing Objectives from Activities

Write an *O* in the blank beside each instructional objective and an *A* beside each activity.

a. _____ The student will discuss in class the reasons for World War I.

b. _____ The student will tell time to the nearest five-minute mark.

c. _____ The student will write a good business letter.

d. _____ The student will read Chapter 3 in the science book and will underline the important things to remember.

e. _____ The student will, with a group of classmates, draw a mural depicting life among the Pilgrims.

You should have marked items b and c as instructional objectives. Items a, d, and e are activities.

You may sometimes have difficulty telling whether an item is an objective or an activity when it is written by someone else. That's because you can't always be certain of the other person's intent. For this reason you may have had difficulty with one or more items above. You won't have this difficulty when working with your own objectives and activities. Just remember that objectives are statements of skills or attitudes that you want students to acquire from instruction and to continue to possess over a period of time. In contrast, activities are the learning experiences in which students participate for the purpose of acquiring the skills.

IDENTIFYING WORTHWHILE OBJECTIVES

Perhaps the easiest way to teach most courses is to give the students a textbook and have them work through it. Easy—yes, but usually not satisfactory. At one time or another most of us have heard students complain that certain subject matter is "not relevant" or that it does not prepare them for "real life." Teachers sometimes make similar judgments. Those of us who carefully analyze textbooks in our teaching fields often think that much of the content is not important enough to teach, while other content that we think is important is omitted.

Deciding what skills or attitudes are important for students to acquire is a major responsibility of every teacher. It is also one that we often overlook or take too lightly because it is so easy to use published materials without giving much thought to their appropriateness. As teachers, we should examine each potential objective for our courses to determine whether it is worthwhile. A good way to do this is simply to answer the following questions about the skill stated in the objective.

1. *Is this a skill that the students will actually use in life?*
2. *If not, is this skill required in order to acquire another useful skill?*

If the answer to either of the above questions about an objective is "yes," then the objective can be considered to be worthwhile.

Exercise 2.3 provides practice in identifying worthwhile outcomes. Answer all items before checking your answers.

EXERCISE 2.3. Identifying Worthwhile Objectives

Look at the pair of objectives below from a unit on phonics for beginning readers. Mark an *X* by the more worthwhile objective of the two. (Be sure to ask the two questions about the worth of each objective.)

1a. _____ The student will select pictures of objects that rhyme (for example, mark the objects that rhyme in pictures of a cat, dog, hat, and bat).

1b. _____ The student will sound out new words composed of letters whose sounds were learned earlier.

Now mark an *X* by the more worthwhile objective of the two below from a primary-grade arithmetic unit on money.

2a. _____ The student will describe how a clerk should make change for purchases of less than a dollar.

2b. _____ The student will tell whether he or she receives the correct change for a dollar when making purchases of less than a dollar.

In the first pair, item 1b is the more worthwhile objective. Sounding out new words is an important skill that young children can use often in reading. However, think again about item 1a—selecting pictures of objects that rhyme. Do you ever do this when you read? Of course not. Nor does selecting such pictures help one to sound out printed words or perform other actual reading tasks. Consequently, this would not be a worthwhile reading objective.

Item 2b—telling whether one received the correct change—is the more worthwhile objective in the second pair. This definitely is a skill that people use regularly. On the other hand, it seems unlikely that most students will actually use the skill in item 2a—describing how a clerk should make change. Of course, actually making change for different types of transactions, as contrasted with describing how to do it, is a crucial skill for persons working as clerks. It would be appropriate to teach this skill to older students who were planning to become store clerks, for example, or to persons in on-the-job clerical training.

MEMORY AND APPLICATION OBJECTIVES

In many instructional situations, the instruction stops short of dealing with the most important objective for the content being taught. Students memorize information but do not apply it appropriately. This may occur, for example, when students learn a definition but do not apply it to a number of examples. Here are two objectives that illustrate this situation.

The student will define each of the eight parts of speech (noun, verb, pronoun, adverb, adjective, preposition, conjunction, and interjection).

The student will identify examples of each part of speech in a passage containing one or more examples of each part.

The first of these objectives is one that merely requires students to give definitions of terms—definitions that can be memorized with little or no understanding. The second objective requires them to identify examples of the content being taught, a skill that they are more likely to use in life and one that demonstrates greater understanding of the

I don't understand it, Ms. Valdez. I memorized all the steps.

content. Both of these objectives can be considered to be worthwhile— the first because it is helpful or required to learn the second; the second because students are likely to use it in later life.

Learning formulas or descriptions of procedures is similar to learning definitions. Ultimately it is the actual use of the formula or set of procedures that will be of most worth to students. An objective that merely requires students to state a formula or describe a set of procedures is worthwhile because it is helpful subsequently in learning to use the formula or procedures. However, objectives that require students to actually use the formula or procedures appropriately are more worthwhile as final objectives. In planning instruction of this type, therefore, you should be sure to develop objectives that require students to perform the actual operations you want them to learn.

Now complete exercise 2.4, which provides practice in identifying worthwhile objectives.

EXERCISE 2.4.   Identifying Worthwhile Objectives

Look at each pair of objectives below. Mark an X by the more worthwhile objective in each pair.

1a. _____ The student will name each example correctly when shown examples of isosceles, scalene, and equilateral triangles.

1b. _____ The student will define each of the three types of triangles (isosceles, scalene, and equilateral).

2a. _____ The student will write the formula for computing the area of a triangle.

2b. _____ The student will compute the area of triangles whose base and height are given.

3a. _____ The student will perform cardiopulmonary resuscitation (CPR) on a mannequin.

3b. _____ The student will describe the procedure for performing cardio-pulmonary resuscitation.

The correct answers are 1a, 2b, and 3a. Each of these items requires students to apply the information contained in a definition, formula, or set of procedures, rather than merely having them state or write the definition, formula, or procedures. Remember, stating or writing the item from memory may also be considered to be a worthwhile objective either in its own right or because it may be necessary in order to subsequently apply the information. The application objectives are more worthwhile as final objectives, however, because they represent more useful skills.

ATTITUDINAL OBJECTIVES

What are the best types of attitude and interest objectives? Ideally, they should describe behaviors that are the best possible indicators that the desired attitudes and interests have been acquired. Verbal statements and responses to questionnaires indicate student attitudes. An even better indicator is behavior in the types of situations in which the attitude is important. For example, you might want to develop positive student attitudes toward reading. Consider the following two objectives.

1. The student will attain a total score on the *Reading Attitude Scale* that falls in the "Favorable" or "Very Favorable" range.
2. The student will read an average of at least one unassigned book per month (nine books total) during the school year.

Something seems to be a little wrong. They all had high scores on the *Attitude Toward School* questionnaire.

The second objective is more worthwhile because it describes a very desirable reading behavior. The first objective is also appropriate, though less worthwhile than the second. Many students might give very favorable responses to the *Reading Attitude Scale* or another questionnaire, yet seldom if ever read any material that is not assigned.

For attitude and interest objectives, it is important to develop objectives that reflect the real-life situation in which the attitude or interest should occur. Objectives that call for improvements as indicated by a questionnaire are worthwhile and are not to be rejected as indicators of attitudes. However, responses to questionnaires are not really the performances that we want to influence when dealing with attitudes or interests. Objectives that call for desired changes in behavior related to the attitudes or interests are most worthwhile, because they indicate actual improvements in performance related to the attitude objectives. Often, behaviors that are direct indicators of attitudes can be used in conjunction with student responses to questionnaires to provide a broader overall indication of student attitudes.

Exercise 2.5 provides practice in identifying worthwhile attitudinal objectives.

EXERCISE 2.5.   Identifying Worthwhile Objectives

Mark an X by the more worthwhile objective in each pair below.

1a. _____ The student will participate in at least one sport in the intramural sports program.
1b. _____ The student will rank intramural sports in the top five among all school-sponsored clubs and activities.

2a. _____ The student will have no unexcused absences or tardies and will submit all course assignments on time.
2b. _____ The student will score 60 or higher on the *School Attitude Survey*, thereby demonstrating a favorable attitude toward school.

Objectives 1a and 2a are the more worthwhile objectives. Each requires behavior in an actual situation that reflects the desired attitude or interest. Objectives 1b and 2b are also appropriate and could be used as objectives related to the particular attitudes indicated, but they are less worthwhile than the alternative objectives. Both items in a pair (for example, 1a and 1b) could be used together, of course, to provide a more comprehensive indication of attitudes toward the particular matter of concern.

Exercise 2.6 gives a final set of items on worthwhile objectives.

EXERCISE 2.6.   Identifying Worthwhile Objectives

Mark an X by the more worthwhile objective in each pair below.

1a. _____ The student will identify the probable liberal vote (yes or no) and the probable conservative vote on each of four federal finance bills.

1b. _____ The student will write definitions for the terms liberal and conservative.

2a. _____ The student will have a positive attitude toward nutrition, as indicated by responses to the *Nutrition Inventory* administered at the close of the nutrition unit.

2b. _____ The student will eat at least the recommended minimum daily number of servings from each of the four food groups, as indicated by a daily food record kept for three days at the close of the nutrition unit.

(Objectives 3a and 3b are reading comprehension objectives.)

3a. _____ The student will identify the illustration that best depicts the meaning of the passage, given any passage from the reading text and three illustrations related to the passage.

3b. _____ The student will describe the passage accurately in his or her own words, given any passage from the reading text.

(Objectives 4a and 4b are driver education objectives.)

4a. _____ The student will change a tire properly.

4b. _____ The student will describe the correct procedure for changing a tire.

The correct answers are 1a, 2b, 3b, and 4a. Item 3 may have been difficult for you. You should have answered it correctly if you asked the question of both items: "Is this skill useful in life?" Seldom, if ever, in everyday life must you select from among three choices an illustration that depicts something you read. It may often be useful, however, to describe what you have read accurately in your own words.

IDENTIFYING WELL-WRITTEN OBJECTIVES

You may derive instructional objectives for your courses either by selecting them from existing sources, such as the course textbook or a local curriculum guide, or by preparing your own set of objectives. Objectives must be stated appropriately in order to be most useful in planning instruction and assessment. Whether you select objectives from existing sources or write your own, it is important to be able to tell if particular objectives are stated in a manner in which they will be most useful.

Two elements of an instructional objective are especially important in determining whether it is well written. These are (1) the description of the expected student performance itself and (2) the description of conditions for assessing the performance.

Some educators consider a third element—a statement of the performance standard for the objective—to also be an important part of a well-written objective. The performance standard indicates how well the student must do on the objective in order for his or her performance to be judged acceptable. For objectives involving a complex product or response (for example, producing an original piece of writing, creating a work of art or a musical score, conducting a scientific experiment, performing a psychomotor task), performance standards describe what must be included in the product or response. The teacher is most concerned about such standards when assessing student performance and when providing instruction and feedback. Because of its importance in the assessment process, this type of standard is dealt with in Chapter 4, Assessment.

For objectives that require the student merely to select correct responses or give very brief answers, performance standards indicate the percentage or number of correct responses (for example, 90 percent correct, 3 out of 4 correct, without error) that will be considered acceptable. You can set realistic standards of this type only after you have had experience "teaching" the objective and collecting assessment data that indicates how well students can be expected to do on it. Until you have done this, you will not have a good basis for knowing what is a reasonable performance level to expect for the objective. The lack of such a performance standard does not affect the teacher's ability to design effective instruction and valid assessment for an objective. Because performance standards of this type are often set arbitrarily and have limited usefulness, instruction on them is not included in this book. If you do find such numerical performance standards to be useful at some point, we urge you not to set them until after you have collected assessment information that indicates what performance levels are reasonable to expect from students.

DESCRIBING STUDENT PERFORMANCE

In writing an instructional objective, it is very important to leave no doubt about the nature of the performance expected from students after instruction. For this reason, *an acceptable objective states what students will be able to do, rather than what they will know or how they will feel.* A statement of what students will be able to *do* enables you to plan instruction that is most appropriate for helping students attain the objective. It also helps you to plan good assessment.

Objectives that describe what students will *know* or what they will *feel* are much less desirable than those that describe what students will do. Such objectives describe internal states or processes that, unlike performance, cannot be directly observed. Anyone wishing to use such an objective to plan instruction and assessment must first attempt to infer the student performance its author had in mind. This process relies on guesswork, which makes it difficult or impossible to use the objective most effectively. Therefore, objectives that describe mental processes or attitudinal states, rather than directly observable student performance, are not considered to be well written.

In writing an objective, the key to stating what students will be able to do is the verb. Here are several examples of verbs used in instructional objectives that describe actual student performances (that is, what students will be able to do): *select, state, name, describe, write, build,* and *draw.* There are many more verbs that indicate student performances that can be observed; only a few are listed here to illustrate the type of verb that describes observable performance. This is the type of verb that must be used in a well-written objective.

Objectives that describe internal states or processes can also be identified by their verbs. Examples of verbs used in such objectives include *know, understand, learn, become familiar with, analyze, appreciate,* and *value.* When you see a verb of this type in an objective, you can immediately classify the objective as not being well written. This is not to say that the internal state or process is not important. A well-written objective, however, must describe what the learner will be able to do—an observable performance instead of an internal state or process.

Exercise 2.7 provides practice in identifying instructional objectives that describe observable student performances. Remember to examine the verb in each objective to determine which it describes: (1) an observable action or (2) an internal mental or attitudinal state.

EXERCISE 2.7. Identifying Performance Descriptions

Mark an X by each objective below that describes an observable student performance. (Be sure to read item 7 carefully.)

1. _____ The student will name the four families of musical instruments (strings, woodwinds, percussion, and brass).

2. _____ The student will know the procedure for locating geographic sites on a world map when given their latitude and longitude.

3. _____ The student will comprehend the general meaning of the Declaration of Independence.

4. _____ The student will truly appreciate Renaissance art.

5. _____ The student will correctly pronounce the new vocabulary words in the third-grade reader.

6. _____ The student will describe the themes of at least three 20th-century American plays.

7. _____ The teacher will describe the procedure for multiplying proper fractions.

8. _____ The student will learn the capitals of all 50 states.

Did you mark items 1, 5, and 6? These are the items that describe student performances that are observable. Items 2, 3, and 4 describe internal states or processes, not observable performances. Item 7 describes a teacher performance, not a student performance, and therefore should not be marked. Item 8 describes a process (learning), not an observable skill that students are expected to possess after instruction.

DESCRIBING PERFORMANCE CONDITIONS

In addition to describing what students will be able to do, a well-written objective states what information or materials, if any, students will be given when they are assessed on the objective. The information or materials given to the student are referred to as the performance conditions, or sometimes simply as the "givens." The italicized portions of the following two objectives are the givens for those objectives.

The student will identify statements of fact and statements of opinion *in newspaper editorials.*

Given the letters of the alphabet in printed form, the student will name each letter.

Note the effect of the givens in each example. In the first example, the nature of the expected student performance would not be clear if the objective ended after the word "opinion" and the given materials (newspaper editorials) were not specified. This objective is an example of one in which the givens are identified in the direct statement of the objective, rather than in a phrase beginning with the word "given." If the givens were not included in the second example, the student would merely be required to say the letters of the alphabet from memory (for example, recite the alphabet), rather than naming each letter in its printed form. Of course, greater student understanding and different instruction is required for students to name each printed letter than for them to merely recite the alphabet.

Whether a statement of givens is appropriate in your objective depends upon the particular objective and your intent. If the students are to be given information or materials to use in performing the behavior called for in the objective, then the givens may be (1) necessary, (2) dependent upon your intent, or (3) inappropriate. Here is an example of each situation, followed by an explanation:

- *Givens necessary:* The student will identify nouns and verbs, given . . . .
- *Givens dependent on intent:* The student will name the four competition swimming strokes.
- *Givens inappropriate:* The student will describe at least three causes of the Civil War.

Givens are necessary in the first of these objectives to indicate what material will contain the nouns and verbs. That is, will the students be given a list of nouns and verbs only, a list containing examples of all parts of speech, simple and complex sentences, or some other type of list or passage containing nouns and verbs? This information is necessary in order to clearly communicate the nature of the expected student performance.

Teacher intent would determine whether the objective "The student will name the four competition swimming strokes" is complete as stated or whether givens should be added to it. If you merely wanted the students to be able to say or write from memory the names of the four strokes—backstroke, breaststroke, butterfly, and crawl or freestyle—the objective is correct as stated. However, if you wanted students to be able to name each stroke while seeing it performed, it would be necessary to add to the objective a statement of givens such as "given filmed examples of each stroke." This statement would change the nature of the objective so that additional instruction and greater student understanding would be required. Most of us would undoubtedly judge the form of this objective with givens to be more worthwhile than the form that merely requires naming the strokes from memory.

Givens are inappropriate for the objective "The student will describe at least three causes of the Civil War" because no special information or materials would be given to the student when assessing performance on this objective. The only materials necessary—paper and pen or pencil— are so obvious that it is not necessary to state them to communicate the meaning of the objective. In fact, objectives are not considered to be well written when the phrase "given paper and pencil" is included in them, because the phrase is unnecessary.

Exercise 2.8 provides practice in identifying objectives that require givens and those for which givens are inappropriate.

EXERCISE 2.8 Identifying Objectives That Require Givens

Two of the four instructional objectives below require statements of givens. Mark an X by each of the two objectives that require givens.

1. _____ The student will swim each of the four competition swimming strokes for a distance of at least 25 feet.
2. _____ The student will insert capital letters and periods appropriately at the beginning and end of each sentence.
3. _____ The student will label the following parts of the human digestive system: salivary glands, esophagus, stomach, pancreas, duodenum, small intestine, and large intestine.
4. _____ The students will write an original example of a simile, a metaphor, and personification.

You should have marked items 2 and 3. They require givens; items 1 and 4 do not. In item 2, the givens are needed to indicate what type of material (e.g., a list of sentences, a paragraph) the student will be given to insert the capital letters and periods in. In item 3, the givens are necessary to indicate what the student will be given to label—for example, a diagram of the body or digestive system, a model, or drawings of the individual parts. In item 1, it would not be necessary to include a statement such as "given a swimming pool" because such a given is so obvious.

Two common errors in writing givens are to state (1) instructional activities or events, rather than materials or information given at the time of assessment, and (2) the type of test item to be given. Here is an example of each type of error.

Instructional activity or event stated: *Given a lesson* on levers, the student will name the three classes of levers.

Type of test item stated: *Given multiple-choice items* on the characteristics of each class of levers, the student will correctly identify the characteristics of each class.

The phrase "Given a lesson" in the first objective above refers to an instructional activity. The phrase "Given multiple-choice items" in the second objective refers to a type of test item. Objectives containing givens of either type are not considered to be well written. Phrases such as "given a unit," "given a lecture," and "given practice" are other examples of givens that are incorrect because they state an instructional activity or event, not materials or information that will be given when performance is assessed.

Exercise 2.9 provides practice in determining whether the givens in an objective are appropriate.

EXERCISE 2.9.   Identifying Appropriate Givens

Mark an *X* beside each objective below that contains an appropriate statement of givens.

1. _____ Given diagrams of the three classes of levers, the student will name the class illustrated in each diagram.
2. _____ Given a week's practice in shooting free throws, the student will make at least 6 of 10 free throws.
3. _____ Given an essay question, the student will describe the significance of the Industrial Revolution.
4. _____ The student will name circles, triangles, rectangles, and squares when shown outline drawings of each.
5. _____ Given an outline map of South America, the student will write in the name of each country outlined.

Items 1, 4, and 5 are the correct choices here. They have appropriate statements of givens. (The statement of givens in item 4 begins with the phrase "when shown.") Items 2 and 3 are inappropriate. Item 2 describes an instructional event (practice). Item 3 indicates a type of test item.

IDENTIFYING WELL-WRITTEN OBJECTIVES

You have seen that a well-written objective has the following characteristics:

- It describes an observable student performance.
- It describes the performance conditions, or givens, during assessment, when such a description is appropriate.

A description of givens is not included in an objective, of course, if no particular materials or information is given to the student when the performance is assessed. Either givens may be stated in a phrase beginning with the word "given," or they may be indicated by identifying the given materials or information in another manner.

Now complete exercises 2.10 and 2.11.

EXERCISE 2.10. Identifying Well-Written Objectives

Mark an X by each objective below that is well written.

1. _____ The student will label the four parts of a flower.

2. _____ Given color photographs of well-known paintings by Picasso, Chagall, Miro, and Dali, the student will name the artist and the title of each painting.

3. _____ The student will describe from memory each of the four steps in the process of cell division.

4. _____ Given paper and pen, the student will write an original business letter in the format specified in class.

Items 2 and 3 are well written. Item 3 does not require a statement of givens. Item 1 is not well written because it does not indicate what students will be given to label—a real flower, a diagram of a flower, the individual parts of a flower, or some other item. Item 4 is not well written because the "given paper and pen" statement is so obvious that it should not be included.

EXERCISE 2.11. Identifying Well-Written Objectives

Mark an X by each objective below that is well written.

1. _____ The student will learn the importance of a balanced diet.

2. _____ Given a lecture-demonstration on magnetism, the student will describe how an electromagnet works.

3. _____ The student will voluntarily participate in at least one school or community service activity during the school year.

4. _____ The student will name the food group (milk, meat, vegetable-fruit, bread-cereal) to which each food in a given list of difficult-to-classify foods belongs.

You should have picked items 3 and 4 for this one. Item 1 is not well written because the verb does not indicate an observable performance. In item 2, the givens are an instructional activity. No givens are required for item 3, which would be an appropriate attitudinal objective for an area such as citizenship or school and community service. Item 4 includes givens (a list of difficult-to-classify foods), even though they are not stated in a phrase preceding the statement of the student performance.

WRITING INSTRUCTIONAL OBJECTIVES

You may derive objectives for your course either by adopting existing objectives or by preparing your own. The easier, but often less satisfactory, way is to adopt objectives contained in materials such as course textbooks, local curriculum guides, and published sets of objectives. However, for many courses a good source of prepared objectives may not be available. You may often be unable to find sources of existing objectives that are satisfactory. In such cases, it will be necessary to prepare your own objectives.

There are advantages to preparing instructional objectives in written form, rather than merely thinking them through. The most important one is that the objectives will then be available for reference when planning instructional activities and assessment. A written set of objectives is also helpful for review and sharing with students when they are preparing for tests covering the objectives. In addition, instructional objectives have become the basis for organized curriculum planning in many schools and school districts. A number of states and local districts have laws or policies requiring each teacher to state in written form the objectives for his or her classes. Although initial attempts at writing good objectives may be time consuming, teachers who are experienced at writing them normally take only a minute or so to write out an objective once they have thought it through.

To write your own instructional objectives, you must first determine (1) what the instructional content (that is, the concepts, principles, processes, and so forth) should be and (2) what students should be able to do with respect to the content. There are several sources for identifying appropriate instructional content for a course or for shorter segments of instruction. Experienced teachers can often simply retain the present content of their courses as the base from which to prepare objectives. Textbooks, curriculum guides, course outlines from other teachers, supplementary instructional materials, and your own subject-matter knowledge are also appropriate sources for identifying content.

Once the instructional content has been identified, you derive instructional objectives by deciding what is important for students to be able to do with respect to the content (that is, the skills and attitudes they will be expected to acquire). At this point you should consider whether each potential objective is worthwhile and what givens, if any, are appropriate during assessment.

The following exercises provide practice in writing instructional objectives under two different types of performance conditions. For the first few items, a general description is given of what you might want your students to learn, and you are asked to write an objective from the description. For the final items, a subject-matter topic is given, and you are to write an objective for the given topic.

Now complete exercise 2.12. Remember to use a verb that describes what the student will *do* and to state the givens, if appropriate. After you complete exercise 2.12, continue with exercises 2.13 through 2.16.

EXERCISE 2.12.   Writing Instructional Objectives

Write an instructional objective for the situation described below.

You want your students to look at paragraphs and know which sentence is the topic sentence in each.

Objective:

To be correct, your objective should have included a performance verb (such as identify, select, mark, or write) and givens (a paragraph or paragraphs). Here are two examples of how it could have been written:

The student will identify the topic sentence(s) in given paragraphs.

Given paragraphs, the student will identify the topic sentence in each.

If your objective contained a verb indicating that the student would identify the topic sentence and givens indicating that paragraphs were provided, consider it correct even if it was stated differently from the above examples.

EXERCISE 2.13. Writing Instructional Objectives

Write an objective for the situation described below.

You want your students to be able to do problems such as the following:

$$
\begin{array}{ccc}
29 & 12 & 77 \\
+37 & +53 & +38 \\
\end{array}
$$

Objective:

You could have written this objective in a number of different ways. A verb such as *add, solve,* or *compute* the answer would be most appropriate for describing student performance. The givens must indicate pairs of two-digit numbers. Here are two of the several ways that the objective could be stated:

The student will add pairs of two-digit numbers correctly.

Given addition problems involving pairs of two-digit numbers, the student will solve the problems.

Note that the first of these examples is shorter and simpler than the second. A short and simple form of an objective is desirable when all the necessary information can be included in such a form.

EXERCISE 2.14. Writing Instructional Objectives

Write objectives for each of the two situations described below.

1. The teacher wants students to have a positive attitude toward drama and to indicate this attitude in some manner other than on an attitude scale.

Objective:

2. The teacher wants students to know how much interest will have to be paid on a simple-interest loan when they are told the principal, rate, and time for the loan.

Objective:

For item 1 it was only necessary for your objective to include an observable student performance that indicates a positive attitude toward drama. Here are some examples of possible objectives for this item:

The student will voluntarily try out for a school play during the year.

The student will watch at least five plays on television during the school year.

The student will voluntarily attend at least two school and/or community plays during the year.

The student will join the Drama Club.

Note that in each example the action on the part of the student was voluntary, rather than being required. This indicates an attitudinal objective rather than a class activity. Therefore, when writing attitudinal objectives, it is a good idea to indicate that the student behavior is voluntary.

For item 2, your objective should have included givens (principal, rate, and time). An example of an appropriate objective for this item is:

The student will compute the interest on simple-interest loans when given the principal, rate, and time.

Of course, the givens for item 2 could be stated at the beginning of the sentence, rather than at the end as they are in the example.

EXERCISE 2.15.   Writing Instructional Objectives

Write an instructional objective for the topic "complete and incomplete sentences." The objective should not involve simply defining the two types of sentences.

Objective:

Your objective must have contained a performance verb. Whether it included givens is optional, depending on what you decided to have students do. Here are some examples of correct answers.

Given a list (or a paragraph) containing complete and incomplete sentences, the student will identify each type (or will indicate in some way whether each sentence is complete or incomplete).

The student will write two complete and two incomplete sentences.

EXERCISE 2.16.   Writing Instructional Objectives

Write an objective for *either one* of the following topics: "applying a tourniquet" or "driving onto the freeway from an on-ramp."

Objective:

Here are examples of appropriate objectives for "applying a tourniquet":

Given a cloth and stick, the student will apply a tourniquet to a classmate's arm (or leg).

The student will describe how to apply a tourniquet.

Variations of the above examples that describe an observable student performance should also be considered correct.

Appropriate objectives for "driving onto the freeway from an on-ramp" include:

The student will describe how to drive onto the freeway from an on-ramp.

The student will drive onto the freeway correctly from an on-ramp.

The student will use the proper procedures when driving onto the freeway from an on-ramp.

Again, variations of these objectives that describe an observable student performance should also be counted as correct.

CONCLUSION

Here again are the skills you should have acquired from this chapter:

- Distinguish between instructional objectives and instructional activities
- Identify worthwhile instructional objectives
- Identify well-written instructional objectives
- Write instructional objectives

These skills should help you to consistently develop good instructional objectives. We also encourage you to use them as the basis for planning competency-based instruction for your classes.

Check yourself to see how well you have learned each skill taught in this chapter by completing the self test on pages 85–87.

ADDITIONAL LEARNING ACTIVITIES

1. Select a textbook, a teacher's guide, or a curriculum outline for an instructional program that does not have well-written instructional objectives. Write a set of instructional objectives for a chapter or unit from the materials. Sets of objectives written in this way may be critiqued and discussed by an instructor, another student, a small group, or an entire class.
2. Select a set of well-written instructional objectives from an instructional program or use the objectives written for activity 1 above. Rate the worth of each objective in the set (1 = worthwhile, 2 = uncertain, 3 = not worthwhile) and have other individuals or small groups also rate the objectives on their own. Compare the ratings of several individuals or groups for the same objectives. Discuss (1) the reasons for different ratings of the same objective and (2) how to deal with such differences when they occur between different teachers, between teachers and students, or between parents and teachers.
3. Read the book entitled *Instructional Objectives* by Popham and others (reference follows), which deals with important issues related to objectives and presents arguments for and against their use. Consider these arguments in deciding whether instructional objectives will be useful to you in teaching. If possible, discuss the arguments in class or with a group of teachers.

   Popham, W. J., Eisner, E. W., Sullivan, H. J., and Tyler, L. L. *Instructional Objectives.* Chicago: Rand McNally, 1969, 142 pp.
4. Study the levels of objectives for the cognitive and/or the affective domain as presented in the handbooks cited here. Either (1) classify a set of objectives, such as those for activities 1 or 2, into the appropriate categories of the taxonomy or (2) write one objective for each level of one of the taxonomies. Sets of objectives written or classified according to one of the taxonomies may be critiqued and discussed in a manner similar to that suggested for activity 1.

   Bloom, B. (Editor). *Taxonomy of Educational Objectives, Handbook I: Cognitive Domain.* New York: David McKay, 1956.

   Krathwohl, D. (Editor). *Taxonomy of Educational Objectives, Handbook II: Affective Domain.* New York: David McKay, 1964.

Chapter 3

EFFECTIVE
INSTRUCTION

Once you've decided what your students should learn, you're ready to think about teaching it. Good instruction follows directly from your objectives. It is the heart of the educational process. Our concerns with the other two elements of CBI—objectives and assessment—are to ensure that instruction deals with important things to learn and that it works.

The purpose of competency-based instruction, of course, is to enable your students to acquire the skills and attitudes reflected in your objectives. Prior to instruction it is assumed or determined through assessment that the students, or at least a high percentage of them, do not possess these competencies. At the conclusion of effective instruction, the students will possess them.

This chapter deals with several elements of effective instruction. It is organized into sections that correspond closely to the parts of a good instructional activity or lesson, as shown here:

- Introducing the activity
- Providing information
- Providing practice
- Providing knowledge of results
- Reviewing the activity

The instructional objectives for this chapter are skills that will help you plan and deliver effective instruction. These objectives, stated as skills you should be able to perform after completing the chapter, are as follows:

- Identify and write appropriate instructional information for given instructional objectives

- Identify and write appropriate student practice activities for given objectives
- Identify activities that provide the most desirable individual student practice and the most desirable amount of practice for given objectives
- Identify appropriate procedures for providing knowledge of results in given instructional situations

INTRODUCING LEARNING ACTIVITIES

In introducing a learning activity, you should perform at least two tasks: (1) communicate the objective to the students and (2) provide a motivator.

When communicating the objective, use language that is easily understood by the students. You should be precise in explaining what is to be learned. If feasible, use examples of the learning tasks, such as sample problems or a demonstration of the performance, as part of the explanation.

In motivating students for the activity, be sure to inform them of the value of what they will be learning. Explain why the knowledge or skill is important in its own right and/or as a necessity for learning other knowledge or skills. It is helpful to relate the usefulness of the new learning to life outside the school, as well as to previous or future school work. Whenever possible, you should also emphasize the importance of the objective for students' immediate needs and interests, rather than for more remote, long-range matters.

PROVIDING INFORMATION

Students learning to perform a new task normally lack basic information essential to performing the task correctly. For example, consider the following objective:

The student will identify the peninsulas on an outline map.

If students are unable to identify peninsulas, it is logical to assume that they do not know their characteristics. The students need a definition of peninsulas or a description of their characteristics in order to identify them correctly. Similarly, if students are to learn to perform an operation or procedure that they cannot presently perform, they need to know the steps involved in the procedure. You must present them with the basic information needed to perform the procedure or have them get this information in some other way.

Presenting the necessary information in a clear and concise manner greatly increases the likelihood that students will be able to use it to perform the task correctly. You should present only the information necessary for learning to perform the task during this initial segment of instruction. Other matters, such as interesting anecdotes and additional, but nonessential, information about the topic, may distract or confuse the student or otherwise interfere with learning. Emphasize the importance of the essential information by presenting it in a straightforward manner, rather than embedding it in other material or breaking it up by discussion or other means. Given this emphasis on the basic information, students are more likely to perceive its importance and to learn it.

Exercises 3.1 and 3.2 provide practice in identifying appropriate information for use in instruction. Remember: *The basic information needed is the definition, description, or set of procedures that will enable students to perform the task stated in the objective.*

EXERCISE 3.1. Identifying Instructional Information

For each objective below, mark an X beside the most appropriate statement for enabling students to perform the task stated in the objective.

1. *Objective*: The student will identify isosceles triangles, given examples of the three types of triangles.

    a. _____ There are three types of triangles: isosceles, equilateral, and scalene.

    b. _____ Triangles are classified into three types: equilateral, isosceles, and scalene. The number of equal sides determines the type of triangle.

    c. _____ An isosceles triangle has two equal sides.

2. *Objective*: The student will read the word "dog." (Note: Other words could also be included in this objective.)

    a. _____ Our story today is about a dog. This is the word "dog" (displays dog flashcard). We'll be reading it a lot in the story, so look closely at it.

    b. _____ This word (displays dog flashcard) is "dog."

    c. _____ This word (displays dog flashcard) is "dog," one of the new words in our story today. How many of you have doggies at home?

Choice c is correct for objective 1 and choice b for objective 2. For objective 1, choice c contains the basic information (an isosceles triangle has two equal sides) that is needed to identify examples of isosceles triangles. Neither of the other two choices contains specific information about the defining characteristics of an isosceles triangle. In order to further clarify the meaning of the information in choice c, it would be appropriate to also provide one or more examples of isosceles triangles with the information.

For objective 2, choice b contains all the information needed to learn to sight read the word "dog." Choices a and c contain this information too, but they also include other material that may divert the student's attention from the basic information to be learned. The other material, particularly that in choice a, would be quite appropriate for use in motivating students during an introductory activity, but it should not be presented at the precise time as the basic instructional information.

EXERCISE 3.2.   Identifying Instructional Information

For each objective, mark an X beside the most appropriate statement for enabling students to perform the task stated in the objective.

1. *Objective*: The student will list the steps in administering mouth-to-mouth resuscitation.

   a. _____ The steps in administering mouth-to-mouth resuscitation are as follows: (here each step would be listed in order).

   b. _____ Mouth-to-mouth resuscitation should be used in cases when the person has stopped breathing or is having difficulty breathing, but the heart is still beating.

2. *Objective:* The student will compute the amount of electrical current, given the voltage and resistance.

   a. _____ Current is measured in amperes, voltage in volts, and resistance in ohms.

   b. _____ Increasing the voltage also increases the current, resulting in a greater number of amperes.

   c. _____ To compute the current, divide the voltage by the resistance.

The correct answers are choice a for objective 1 and choice c for objective 2. These choices contain the basic information needed to perform the tasks stated in their respective objectives. The information in the other choices for each of the two objectives could also be presented during the instructional sequence, but not precisely at the time that students are being taught to perform the specific tasks stated in the objective.

Exercises 3.3 and 3.4 involve the somewhat more difficult task of writing the information for given objectives.

Exercise 3.3.   Providing Information

Write the information you would provide to enable students to perform the task stated in the following objective.

Objective: The student will identify peninsulas on an outline map.

Information:

Appropriate information for the objective would be a statement such as "A peninsula is a body of land almost completely surrounded by water" or "A peninsula is a land mass surrounded on three sides by water." This is the type of information that a student would need in order to be able to correctly identify peninsulas. One or more examples of peninsulas could also be presented, if you feel that the use of examples with the information would help students to subsequently identify peninsulas.

Exercise 3.4.   Providing Information

Objective: The student will compute the average for a given set of numbers.

Information:

You could use statements such as the following to provide the information needed for the objective:

Add the numbers. Divide the total by the number of numbers you added.

Add the numbers to get the total. Count the number of numbers you added. Divide the total by the number of numbers.

Your answer is correct if it is similar to one of these two statements.

For information that is potentially difficult to understand without examples or sample problems, such as in the above statements, provide examples or sample problems and explain or work through them with the students. For many objectives, there may be no way to state the information so simply that it can be used without one or more examples to perform the task correctly. In such cases, use examples as needed to supplement the basic information.

There are a limited number of concepts that can be taught more effectively simply by using examples of the particular concepts without describing their characteristics. Teaching of a concept by examples only is appropriate when you find it difficult or impossible to define the concept in language that your students will understand. A number of such difficult-to-define concepts are often found in preschool and kindergarten curricula. For instance, colors, shapes, and sizes are concepts that are very difficult to define but are teachable by examples. The "information" that is provided in teaching a concept from these categories consists of examples and non-examples of the concept, with each example and non-example being appropriately identified. Consider the following objective:

The students will identify red objects when shown red and non-red objects.

To provide information for this objective, you would simply display first a variety of red objects and tell the pupils "These are red" and then a number of objects of other colors (for example, green block, orange ball, and yellow pencil) and say "These are not red." Thus, you would present the information that pupils need to attain the objective exclusively in the form of examples of the concept, rather than by a definition or description. A similar procedure would be used to provide

In summary, class, just remember this simple little rule: Ontogeny recapitulates phylogeny.

appropriate instructional information for any other concept being taught by examples only.

The instructional information you present to students when they are learning to perform a new task should be simple and straightforward. You should explain the procedure or operation to be performed by students in the simplest possible manner. When you use examples, take care to select ones that are easy to understand. For instance, in providing examples for computing the average of a set of numbers, you might decide to use only a few one-digit numbers for the first example. If you give students "tough" examples early, it is likely to hinder their effort to learn to perform the task. Also, if you tell them other ways to perform a task before they have thoroughly mastered the simplest way, they may become hopelessly confused. In short, keep it as simple as possible.

PROVIDING APPROPRIATE PRACTICE

We are all familiar with the value of practice. "Practice makes perfect" is a common saying that gives testimony to the need for practice, and "We learn by doing" has been a byword among educators for decades. Providing students with opportunities to practice what we want them to learn is one of the most important parts of the instructional process.

As teachers, we may sometimes lose sight of the value of practice. We may simply lecture to students or have them read portions of a textbook, and then test them on their knowledge of the content and/or their ability to apply it. In such cases no practice is given on the tasks on which students are tested. This method of "instruction" is sure to yield less student learning and poorer test performance than when we provide direct practice.

Consider for a moment the inappropriateness of assessing students on tasks that they have not had an opportunity to practice. Recall the objective from intermediate-grade arithmetic used earlier:

The student will identify isosceles triangles, given examples of the three types of triangles.

Providing students with the information "An isosceles triangle has two equal sides" is a necessary step to enable them to identify isosceles triangles. However, for many students this information alone will not be sufficient. They will need practice in which they are presented with each of the three types of triangles and are asked to identify the isosceles. That is, they will need practice on the task stated in the objective, in addition to being provided with the needed information.

This practice, accompanied by feedback on whether each practice response is correct, is likely to result in greatly improved performance.

Appropriate practice is practice of the exact task stated in the objective. Thus, if your objective calls for "identifying isosceles triangles, given examples of the three types of triangles," the practice you provide will involve identifying isosceles triangles from among examples of the three types. Both the student performance required and the givens will be identical to those stated in the objective.

Exercises 3.5 and 3.6 contain items in which you identify appropriate practice activities for given objectives.

EXERCISE 3.5. Identifying Appropriate Practice

Mark an X beside the activity that is most appropriate for providing practice related to the objectives below.

1. *Objective*: The student will read the new words from each story contained in the first-grade reading book.

    a. _____ The children act out each story to increase their comprehension of the new words and the story.

    b. _____ For each story, the teacher asks oral comprehension questions that include the new words and the children answer the questions.

    c. _____ The children use cut-out letters to make the new words from each story and to increase their perceptual abilities.

    d. _____ The children are shown the new words from each story individually on flashcards and are asked to read each word.

2. *Objective*: The student will compute the amount of interest on any simple-interest loan, given the principal, interest rate, and time period for the loan.

    a. _____ Students complete a worksheet containing problems in which any three of the four loan factors (principal, interest rate, time period, and amount of interest) are given for several different simple-interest loans. The students compute the amount of the factor that is not given.

    b. _____ A banker is invited to visit the class as a guest speaker. She explains simple-interest loans to the students; then she demonstrates how to calculate the amount of interest for different principal amounts, interest rates, and time periods.

    c. _____ Students complete a worksheet containing problems in which the principal, interest rate, and time period are given for several different simple-interest loans. Students compute the amount of interest for each loan.

d. _____ Students are asked to obtain the relevant information, including principal, interest rate, time periods, and amount of interest, about a simple-interest loan actually made to their parents or some other individual(s). Each student is asked to explain how the interest for his or her particular loan was computed.

You should have marked choice d for item 1 and choice c for item 2. For item 1, choice d is the only activity in which children practice the task stated in the objective—reading the new words. The other choices are activities that do not require the children to read the words. For item 2, choice c is the only activity with the same student performance and givens as contained in the objective. The activity in choice a would require the students to compute each of the four factors, rather than only the amount of interest. Choice b does not require student practice of a task. In choice d, all four factors are given in the loan information, and the student simply has to explain how the given interest amount was computed for the loan.

EXERCISE 3.6.   Identifying Appropriate Practice

For each objective below, mark an X beside the activity that is most appropriate for providing practice related to the objective.

1. *Objective*: Given printed advertisements, the students will name the type(s) of advertising appeal(s) used in each.

   a. _____ Students are asked to write the name of each type of advertising appeal and, for each appeal, to write a sample advertisement about a real or fictitious product.
   b. _____ Students are given printed advertisements from newspapers or magazines and are asked to write the name of each type of appeal used in each advertisement.
   c. _____ Students are given printed advertisements from newspapers and magazines and the names of each type of advertising appeal. Students are asked to write beneath each advertisement the name of each appeal used in it.
   d. _____ Students are asked to bring to class one or more printed advertisements illustrating each type of advertising appeal.

2. *Objective*: The students will write a descriptive essay of at least 300 words.

   a. _____ Have each student choose a topic and write an essay describing it.
   b. _____ Have the students read several examples of good descriptive essays.
   c. _____ Write a descriptive essay as a class activity by calling on a different student to contribute each new sentence.
   d. _____ Have each student orally describe an unknown object of the student's choice until the other students can guess what the object is.

Choice b is correct for item 1 and choice a for item 2. For item 1, the activity in choice b is the only one in which printed advertisements are given and the students themselves are required to name each type of appeal used. In choice c, both the names of the appeals and the advertisements are given, so that students are not required to know or supply the name of each type of appeal. For item 2, choice a is correct because it is the only activity in which the student is required to write a complete essay, as stated in the objective.

Now try exercises 3.7 and 3.8, which require you to write practice activities that would be appropriate for given objectives. When writing a practice activity for an objective, be sure to indicate both the form of the materials (for example, flashcards, list of words, story, or transparencies), if any, to be used in the activity and the nature of the student responses. That is, don't just paraphrase the statement in the objective. Describe the activity briefly, but in enough detail so that the form of the materials, if any, and of the student responses is clear.

EXERCISE 3.7. Providing Appropriate Practice

Write an activity that would provide appropriate practice for the objective below.

Objective: The student will identify the topic sentences in given paragraphs.

Activity:

For any appropriate practice activity for the objective, you would give the students a number of paragraphs (for example, on a worksheet, in a book, or projected from transparencies). You would ask them to indicate the topic sentence of each paragraph using any means that is convenient to use and easy for you or the student to check (for example, draw brackets around it, underline it, asterisk the first word, or write a number to indicate its position in the paragraph). Thus, your answer is correct if your activity involved giving the students several paragraphs in a specified form (for example, on a worksheet) and having them indicate the topic sentences by a means such as those just noted.

EXERCISE 3.8.   Providing Appropriate Practice

Write an activity that would provide appropriate practice for the objective below.

Objective: Given any one-digit numeral, the student will construct a set of objects corresponding to the given numeral.

Activity:

For this activity you would give students the numeral in a specified form (orally or on a flashcard). They would be required to count out or display, from among objects available to them (crayons, pencils, sheets of paper, or books), the corresponding number of objects. Your description of the activity should have included the form in which the numeral would be given and the type(s) of objects that would be used for the activity. Note that, because only the numeral is given, this is not an activity in which students would match given numerals with given sets of objects. Rather, they would count out each set of objects themselves.

The amount of practice needed to perform a task well typically increases with the complexity of the task. Most students are unlikely to be able to learn at one time all of the information needed to perform a complex task and to correctly apply the information in practicing the complete task. Thus, if the task involves several steps, students normally will learn more efficiently if you first have them practice the steps individually or in related sets. Then you can also provide the instructional information and the feedback on the correctness of practice responses for each smaller set of steps, rather than for the entire task at once. After students learn the component steps, you can combine the steps so that students practice the complete task.

It is very important to perceive your role as a teacher as one in which you provide conditions that help *all* students learn as well as possible, rather than one in which you simply make information and resources available for students to learn according to their abilities. If you present the information for performing a task but do not provide appropriate practice, the top students may still perform quite well because of their better ability to interpret and apply the information. Less able students, however, are unlikely to be able to perform the task without an opportunity to practice it. Good instruction will include practice of the exact task stated in the objective because such practice helps students learn.

PROVIDING INDIVIDUAL AND FREQUENT PRACTICE

Practice really makes a difference. So does the type of practice we give students. For instruction to be most effective, students should have the opportunity to practice individually and often.

INDIVIDUAL PRACTICE

One important consideration in instruction is to ensure that all students have the opportunity for individual practice on an objective. Observation of classroom teaching has revealed that, in many oral practice activities, practice often is not evenly distributed among individual students. For example, teachers call upon students who already know the answers more frequently than those who are having difficulty, volunteers more often than nonvolunteers, and girls more frequently than boys. Thus, some individuals, often those who need it most, receive less practice than their classmates on the things they are expected to learn.

You can help to ensure more equal and active participation by your students in oral practice activities if you use a few simple guidelines for individual practice. The following guidelines for calling on students should help you to conduct effective oral practice activities.

1. *Distribute individual practice evenly across all students, but do not use a detectable pattern that will enable students to know who will be called on next.*
2. *Call on:*
   - *Boys as often as girls*
   - *Nonvolunteers as often as volunteers*
   - *Individuals more frequently than groups*
   - *Students who are having learning difficulties as often as those who are not*
3. *Allow time for all students to think of an answer before calling on an individual by name.*

There is a reason, of course, for each of these guidelines. The purpose of distributing practice evenly across all students is to give each student a relatively equal number of opportunities to practice. A detectable pattern of calling on students should be avoided because it permits a student to participate by paying attention only when his or her turn is near. The guideline regarding calling on individuals from different groups (for example, boys/girls and nonvolunteers/volunteers) a similar number of times is another procedure for distributing practice evenly across all students, in order to avoid falling into the common patterns of unequal distribution of practice that occur in many classrooms. Group responding in oral practice should not be used too frequently because many students do not respond at all when the entire group is called upon. Others simply echo the response of the first student or two who answer, without actually thinking through both the question and the answer themselves. Calling on an individual by name *after* students have had time to think of the answer to a question, rather than before the question is asked or time is allowed to think of the answer, will help ensure that the other students pay attention. The students will not know that the question is not directed to them until after they have had time to think of the answer.

Now try the items in exercise 3.9 to see how well you can apply the guidelines on individual practice.

This group practice is great. My arithmetic isn't better, but I'm getting good at lipreading.

EXERCISE 3.9. Identifying Individual Practice

Mark an X by the correct choice for each item below.

1. Which activity would be best for the objective "The students will be able to give good descriptive talks"?

   a. _____ Have each student plan a descriptive talk. To avoid excessive use of class time, select at random a limited number of students to actually give their talks to the class.

   b. _____ Have each student plan a descriptive talk and give it to the class.

   c. _____ Have each student plan a descriptive talk in order to provide the practice for all students. Make giving of the talks optional for each student so as to spare shy and limited-ability students the discomfort of actually giving the talk.

   d. _____ Select students who will serve as models of good speaking behavior and who can speak easily to a group. Have them individually plan and present descriptive talks.

2. Which procedure would be best for calling on students during oral practice?

   a. _____ Call on students without using any fixed pattern, placing checks on a list of names to see that all students are called upon about an equal number of times.

   b. _____ To provide the maximum opportunities for practice, usually call on the entire group or class to respond together.

   c. _____ To keep the number of turns equal for all students, call on individual students in order as listed in your class roll book.

   d. _____ Call exclusively on children who are having difficulty with the learning task, because they need the most practice.

3. Which question below would be the best way to call for a response during an oral practice activity?

   a. _____ "What is this . . . Vernon?"   c. _____ "Vernon . . . what is this?"
   b. _____ "Who would like to tell   d. _____ "What is this?"
              me what this is?"

The correct choices are b for item 1, a for item 2, and a for item 3. For item 1, b is the correct choice because it is the only one in which all students practice the task of giving a descriptive talk. Thus, appropriate practice for the objective is distributed across all students. For item 2, a is correct because it is the only choice in which practice is distributed across all students without a detectable pattern being used. Choice a is correct in item 3 because time is allowed for students to think of the answer before an individual student is called upon. Choice b is less desirable than a because the question calls for students to volunteer, and choice d is less desirable than a because it permits volunteer or group responses.

FREQUENT PRACTICE

Practice activities are often designed to provide either initial student practice on an objective or review for one or more objectives. These activities will be most effective when you arrange conditions so that as many students as possible have a high rate of individual practice throughout the activity. High rates of individual practice are obtained when individual students answer each item on their own during the same time period and when students work in pairs and alternately answer sets of items individually. Such activities involving high individual response rates for all students are far preferable to those in which only one student in the group or class is responding at a given time or in which the students are responding as a group. That is, you should maximize the rate of individual practice that all students receive during an activity. A good guideline to use for providing the most desirable amount of practice is as follows:

Provide as high a rate of individual practice as possible for each student during the activity. Avoid factors that unnecessarily reduce the individual practice rate.

Now try your hand at applying this guideline by working through exercise 3.10.

EXERCISE 3.10.   Identifying Frequent Practice

Mark an X by the correct choice for each item below.

1. Which activity below would provide the most frequent practice for the objective "The students will classify given foods into the correct groups from the four food groups"?

    a. _____ Place cards, each containing an illustration of a particular food, face down on a table. Have a student come to the table, pick a card, display it, and name the food group to which it belongs. Call on other individual students, without using any fixed pattern, to repeat this process.

    b. _____ Group the students in pairs. Give each pair a set of cards with a food shown on the front side and the name of the food and its food group on the back. Have the two students in each pair drill each other by showing their partner the food and having the partner name the food group.

    c. _____ Distribute a few food cards face down to each student. Ask any student to select a card, display it, and name the food group for the food illustrated on it. Then have the next student in the row (or at the same table) repeat this procedure. Continue around the room in the same manner.

d. _____ Call on students individually, without using a fixed pattern, to name the food group for each food as you display food cards one at a time. Be sure that all students are called on about an equal number of times.

2. Which activity would provide the most desirable amount of practice for the objective "The student will multiply one-digit numbers by 5"?

a. _____ Have each student practice writing out each multiplication fact as a related addition fact (for example, $3 \times 5 = 5 + 5 + 5 = 15$).

b. _____ Hold up flashcards of the 5s and call on the entire class to give the products.

c. _____ Give each student a worksheet consisting of story problems which involve multiplying one-digit numbers by 5.

d. _____ Give each student a worksheet consisting of multiplication fact problems which involve multiplying one-digit numbers by 5.

The correct answers are choice b for item 1 and choice d for item 2. For item 1, choice b is correct because the activity enables half of the students to classify the foods at one time, while the other students also are participating as "teachers." Thus, this activity provides the highest rate of individual practice. Choice d is correct for item 2 because the activity enables all students to practice the task of multiplying one-digit numbers by 5 individually and at the same time. The activity in choice b involves class responding, rather than individual practice; and the activity in choice c is based on story problems, which yield a much lower response rate because they require time to read and understand.

PROVIDING KNOWLEDGE OF RESULTS

Knowledge of results, or feedback as it is often called, is information given to students about the correctness of their responses. You may provide knowledge of results for your students in very simple form, such as by making a checkmark to indicate incorrect answers or by saying "yes" or "good" for correct oral responses and by saying "no" or by giving the correct answer for incorrect oral responses. You may also supply it in much more detailed form, such as by providing a complete explanation of why a particular answer is correct or incorrect.

Research indicates that knowledge of results is often effective in helping students learn. It is natural for us as teachers to give feedback on student performance, especially when students answer incorrectly, but often we simply respond instinctively without giving much thought to the nature of the feedback we are providing. The form and manner in

Would you be interested in knowing where you went wrong, Gridley?

which feedback is given, however, are important in determining its effectiveness.

Providing knowledge of results for oral practice activities involving factual information is a relatively simple matter. Here are the procedures to use in such situations:

- When the student answers correctly: *Make a brief positive remark (for example, "Good," "That's right," or "Very good, Carol").*
- When the student answers incorrectly or does not answer: *Tactfully give the correct answer. Then repeat the item and have the same student answer it.*
- When the student is hesitant and you feel some help is in order: *Give a choice of the correct answer and a feasible incorrect one ("Is it . . . or . . . ?").* Do not use more elaborate hints than this. If the student answers the two-choice prompt incorrectly, use the procedure for incorrect answers.

What are the reasons for each of these procedures? In the case of the student who answers correctly, it is to affirm to the group that the answer is correct and to positively acknowledge the student's success. For the student who answers incorrectly or does not respond, it is to provide the correct answer and to give the student an opportunity to practice answering the item correctly. When the student is asked to answer the item after you supply the correct answer initially, the student should look at and/or hear the item again. In this way he or she must associate the answer with the question instead of simply echoing the answer you gave. When you provide prompts (hints), you should use only very direct ones that have a high likelihood of yielding the correct answer. One study of hints provided by teachers under normal classroom conditions revealed that the hints resulted in correct answers less than 20 percent of the times they were used. Further, students often redirect their attention from the question itself to the hint, so that they do not make the desired association between the question and their answer, even if it is correct.

Now try to apply the procedures for providing knowledge of results by answering the items in exercise 3.11.

EXERCISE 3.11.   Providing Knowledge of Results

Mark an X by the correct choice for each item below.

1. You have just called on Susan to read the word "saw." She says "was." Which procedure would be best for providing knowledge of results?

   a. _____ Have Susan look at the word again. Say "It's something we use to cut wood, Susan. Now try it again."

   b. _____ Call on another member of the class to read the word. Then have Susan say it.

   c. _____ Say "No, Susan, but you're close. You just reversed the letters. Now look at it closely and try it again."

   d. _____ Have Susan look at it again. Say "It's 'saw,' Susan. Now you read it."

2. Ricardo has just given a correct answer. Which of the following would be best to say?

   a. _____ "That's right, Ricardo." Then explain why his answer is correct.

   b. _____ "Good work, Ricardo. You got it right so you may call on the next person."

   c. _____ "Good, Ricardo."

   d. _____ "Very good, Let's see if you can get two in a row."

You should have marked choice d for item 1 and choice c for item 2. Choice d is correct for item 1 because it is the only choice in which the teacher has Susan look at the word, gives the correct answer, and then has Susan try the answer again. For item 2, choice c is correct because a brief positive remark to affirm the student's response is the appropriate feedback for a correct answer.

The guidelines for knowledge of results for written work are, of course, different from those for oral activities. Here they are:

1. *Comment on the papers.* For routine brief assignments and short-answer exercises, it is not necessary to comment on the majority of the papers. However, for such items as longer reports and essays, you should make comments like the following on every paper.

- A positive written comment when the student has done well
- An encouraging, but honest, comment if you feel the student tried hard, even if the paper is not a particularly good one
- Tactful and explicit suggestions for improvement on all papers for which students can make appropriate improvements

2. *Mark and return the papers quickly.* For longer papers that may contain many errors (for example, essays), limit your marking or corrections to a few types of errors, especially on the papers of students who make a large number of mistakes. Concentrate on errors related to the instructional objective(s) for which the paper was assigned and on the other most common major errors made by each student. If you mark an enormous number of errors on a long written paper, it may befuddle and demoralize the student to the point where the feedback is of little or no value. (Be sure to tell the class the procedure you used in marking the papers.) Keep a list of the few most common types of errors made by the class, so that you can refer to them and have the students look for them in their own work when you review the papers.

3. *Review the papers.* For short-answer papers, briefly give each correct answer to the students. For papers such as long reports and essays, focus the review on the most common major errors that you noted in marking the papers.

4. *Have the students correct their errors.* Whenever it is feasible, have the students correct their errors. For short-answer items, do this by having the students read or hear each question and write the answer, so that they make the association between the correct answer and the question. For long papers, have them correct the major errors of the type that you marked on their papers. Normally, it is not worthwhile to have the students, especially the lower-ability ones, attempt to find and correct all of the unmarked errors on their papers.

Here then is a brief summary of the procedures you should use for providing knowledge of results on students' written work:

1. Comment.	3. Review.
2. Mark and return quickly.	4. Have students correct errors.

Now try exercise 3.12.

EXERCISE 3.12. Providing Knowledge of Results

Mark an X by the correct choice for each item below.

1. You are teaching a short unit on sentence fragments and run-on sentences. The final objective for this unit is "The student will write essays that contain no sentence fragments or run-on sentences." Near the end of the unit you assign an essay with a minimum length of 500 words. Which is the best procedure below for providing knowledge of results?

   a. _____ Mark everything that is incorrect, including the sentence fragments and run-on sentences. Return and review the papers.

   b. _____ Mark everything that is incorrect, including the sentence fragments and run-on sentences. Return and review the papers. Have each student whose paper contained any errors rewrite the paper.

   c. _____ Mark only the sentence fragments and run-on sentences, plus the other most common major errors made by each student. Return and review the papers. Have the students rewrite the papers, correcting the errors that are marked and all other errors that they detect themselves.

   d. _____ Mark only the sentence fragments and run-on sentences, plus the other most common errors made by each student. Return and review the papers. Have the students rewrite the sentence fragments and run-ons, plus all other errors that you marked, so that they are correct.

2. Your students have submitted comprehensive reports of an experiment as one activity for the objective "The student will write accurate reports of scientific experiments." Which of the following choices best describes the reports on which you should write suggestions for improvements?

   a. _____ All reports for which you can suggest appropriate improvements.

   b. _____ Reports that contain the most common errors made by the class.

   c. _____ All reports that are not particularly good ones—that is, those that have the most room for improvement.

   d. _____ Reports of the students who clearly tried hard on the assignment, even if their reports are not particularly good.

The correct answers are choice d for item 1 and choice a for item 2. For item 1, choice d is the right answer because the students correct only the errors indicated by the teacher, rather than also trying to find and correct all of the unmarked errors, as would be the case in choice c. For item 2, choice a is correct because suggestions for improvement should be made on all papers on which students can make appropriate improvements.

REVIEWING THE ACTIVITY

A good way to conclude an instructional activity is with a brief review or summary of the important points covered in it. You should at least remind students once again of what they learned to do in the activity— that is, you should paraphrase the instructional objective in easily understood language. It is also a good idea to review the key instructional information that was presented. A reminder of why the new learning is important and/or how it is used in real-life situations is also a worthwhile element to include in the review. You may present this summary information yourself or have students give it in response to questions you ask. Students often pay closer attention if they are asked to do the summarizing themselves.

CONCLUSION

The skills covered in this chapter provide a basis for helping you to plan and deliver effective instruction. The chapter covers the basic parts of a well-planned lesson or instructional activity, including (1) introducing the activity, (2) providing information, (3) providing practice, (4) providing knowledge or results, and (5) reviewing the activity. The skills that you should have acquired from the chapter relate to providing students with appropriate instructional information, practice opportunities, and knowledge of results. Your use of these skills in the classroom will help your students to be highly competent learners.

Now check to see how well you have learned the skills taught in this chapter. Complete the self test on pages 90-93.

ADDITIONAL LEARNING ACTIVITIES

1. From among the objectives used as examples in this book or from any other source, select one or more well-written instructional objectives from your own teaching field. Describe how you would teach the objective(s) to a group of students. For each objective, include at least the following:

   a. An appropriate statement of information for enabling students to perform the task stated in the objective
   b. Practice activities that provide appropriate individual practice for the objective

2. Obtain the teacher's edition of a textbook for a content area and grade level with which you are familiar. Do the following:
    a. Analyze the adequacy of the information, the practice, and the feedback provided in the text.
    b. Describe how a teacher could supplement the text to overcome any inadequacies.
    Discuss the analyses and the suggestions for supplemental activities with others.
3. Observe instruction in a classroom or review a transcript or videotape of a class session. Analyze the instruction, practice, feedback, and review. Discuss with others what could be done to increase the effectiveness of the instruction.
4. One of the major concerns regarding minimal competency testing programs is that competency tests may lack curriculum validity—students do not receive instruction on the objectives assessed on the test. Obtain the following instructional materials from a teacher, school, or school district that has a minimal competency testing program: a set of instructional objectives used in the program, the district competency test or other test used to assess performance on the objectives, and the instructional materials for the objectives.

    Prepare an index that shows which materials are related to each objective. If there are objectives for which there are no instructional materials, discuss how these discrepancies can be resolved.

Chapter 4

ASSESSMENT

Following the guidelines described in the preceding chapter should help you teach more effectively. But once you've done your teaching, you'll want to know just how effective it was. Did the students learn what you intended? How well? Here's where assessment comes in. Good competency-based assessment procedures will provide the answers to these questions. You'll know just how well your students are able to perform on what you taught.

Assessment is the third and final major element of competency-based instruction. You will be able to use the results of good assessment procedures to tell how well students can perform on each objective, to identify students who need additional instruction, and to evaluate and improve the effectiveness of your instruction. You will be confident that you are using assessment that is valid and fair because it will be based directly on your own objectives and instruction—that is, on what your students were taught.

The overall purpose of this chapter is to teach you to write good assessment items for your instructional objectives. When you have completed it, you should be able to carry out the following objectives:

- Identify appropriate assessment items for given instructional objectives
- Identify well-written items
- Write good assessment items for instructional objectives

Before going on, we want to say a few words about the title for this chapter, Assessment. Assessment can be a very broad topic. However, this chapter intentionally deals only with the basic content of competency-based assessment that relates to the three instructional objectives above. We've included only what we thought would be most useful to you as a teacher. In contrast, the broader field of educational tests and measurement has been the subject of many comprehensive and sophisticated books. In no way did we intend in this chapter to provide a thorough treatment of measurement principles, practices, or issues. If you want more information on this topic than is provided in this chapter, you may refer to one or more of the numerous textbooks in the educational measurement field.

IDENTIFYING APPROPRIATE ASSESSMENT ITEMS

The assessment items that you write for your instructional objectives are used to determine whether students have acquired the skills and attitudes reflected in the objectives. These items, then, must assess the exact performances called for in the objectives. The conditions, or givens, in an objective must also be included in the assessment. The relationship between the objective and the assessment items is an important concern. Whether the desired relationship exists can be determined by asking two questions:

Wha'da ya mean, *remove* my appendix! I thought I was just supposed to know where it's located!

1. *Does the assessment item require the same performance of the student as that specified in the instructional objective?*
2. *Does the assessment item provide the same conditions or givens as those specified in the instructional objective?*

If the answer to both of these questions is "yes," then the assessment item is appropriate for the objective. If the answer to either question is "no," the assessment is not appropriate. Inappropriate items should be rewritten to achieve the desired relationship with the objective.

Exercises 4.1 and 4.2 provide practice in determining if the performance and the givens in an assessment item are consistent with those specified in the instructional objective. Answer all of the items before checking your answers against those following the exercises.

EXERCISE 4.1. Identifying Appropriate Assessment Items

Mark an X if the assessment items are appropriate for the objectives listed.

1. _____ *Objective:* The student will demonstrate the appropriate procedure for administering cardiopulmonary resuscitation.
   Assessment item: Describe each step in the procedure for administering cardiopulmonary resuscitation, as shown in the illustrations below. (A set of sequenced illustrations is given.)
2. _____ *Objective:* The student will name the food group (milk, meat, vegetable-fruit, bread-cereal) to which each food in a given list of foods belongs.
   Assessment item: List at least three foods in each of the following food groups: milk, meat, vegetable-fruit, bread-cereal.
3. _____ *Objective:* Given the letters *l*, *m*, and *n*, the students will say the sound of each letter.
   Assessment item: The teacher shows the letters *l*, *m*, and *n* individually and calls on the student to "say the sound of this letter."
4. _____ *Objective:* Given descriptions of situations where constitutional rights have been denied, the student will name the rights denied in each situation.
   Assessment item: The student is asked to describe in writing situations from American history in which each of the following constitutional rights has been denied: right to worship, right of peaceful assembly, and right to vote.

The assessment described in number 3 is appropriate because the performance and the givens in the assessment are the same as those in the objective. The items in numbers 1, 2, and 4 are inappropriate. Neither the performance nor the givens included in these items are the same as those specified in the objectives.

EXERCISE 4.2. Identifying Appropriate Assessment Items

Mark an *X* if the assessment items are appropriate for the objectives listed.

1. _____ *Objective*: Given pictures of simple levers, the student will name from memory each type of lever pictured.
   Assessment item: Match the type of lever named in column A with the appropriate lever pictured in column B. (Column A is a list of lever names: first class, second class, and third class. Column B contains pictures of simple levers: can opener, wheelbarrow, broom, shovel, paper cutter, and others.)

2. _____ *Objective*: The student will state the time shown on a clock to the nearest five minutes.
   Assessment item: Teacher sets the hands on a geared demonstration clock and asks the student, "What time is showing on the clock?"

3. _____ *Objective*: The student will identify pairs of objects that are the same size.
   Assessment item: Teacher gives the student pairs of objects that are different in size, then asks the student to "point to the bigger object in each pair."

4. _____ *Objective*: The student will add proper fractions with like denominators.
   Assessment items: Solve the following problems.

$$\frac{1}{5}+\frac{2}{5}= \qquad \frac{1}{6}+\frac{1}{6}= \qquad \frac{3}{8}+\frac{2}{8}= \qquad \frac{1}{9}+\frac{4}{9}=$$

The assessment items in numbers 2 and 4 are appropriate for the objectives listed. The performances required in the assessment items are the same as those stated in the objectives. The givens (a clock in number 2 and proper fractions with like denominators in number 4) are also the same as those specified in the objectives. The assessment items for numbers 1 and 3 are inappropriate. The objective in number 1 does not indicate that the names of the levers are given (the student will name them from memory, according to the objective), but the names are given in the assessment. The objective in number 3 requires the student to identify pairs of objects that are the *same* size, but the assessment item asks the student to identify the *bigger* object.

IDENTIFYING WELL-WRITTEN ASSESSMENT ITEMS

When you are assessing student learning, certain characteristics of your assessment items are especially important. The items should be clearly written so that students understand exactly what is expected of them. The items should not contain prompts or clues that enable the student to respond correctly without having previously learned the correct answers. Learning to detect problems involving clarity and prompting will help you write better items.

Your assessment items should clearly indicate the nature of the response that is expected from the student. When your students are unsure about what is expected, their responses may not accurately reflect their knowledge related to an item. The most common cause of unclear assessment items involves stating the items in a manner that permits more than one interpretation of what is expected.

There are many causes for assessment items not being clearly written. Following are some common practices that result in lack of clarity.

• Asking students to answer questions or follow directions that are unnecessarily complex. Unnecessary complexity may be due to the amount of information included in the item, to poor grammar, or both. The following example illustrates the problem.

The four food groups provide all of the nutrients needed for healthy bodies. Name them.

This item can be written more clearly as a straightforward statement:

Name the four food groups.

• Asking students to fill in completion items where several correct words can be used. For example, the following item can be answered correctly with several different words.

Pacific Ocean salmon spawn in _____.

Correct answers include fresh water, rivers, the fall, pairs, the Northwestern States. The problem of multiple correct answers to a completion item can be avoided by rewriting the item into a straightforward question. The above item is more clearly stated in question form below.

In what type of water do Pacific Ocean salmon spawn?

• Asking students to place things in order without indicating the basis for the ordering. There are many different ways to order things: chronologically, alphabetically, by importance, or by size. The basis for ordering things should be specified in the assessment item.

• Asking students to describe things without indicating the nature of the description that is desired. Most things can be described in at least two ways: by their physical features or by their functions. Assessment items should indicate both what is to be described and what is to be included in the description.

Exercise 4.3 provides practice in identifying clearly written items. Check each item to see if any of the problems just mentioned are present.

EXERCISE 4.3.   Identifying Clearly Written Items

Mark an X by each assessment item that is clearly written.

1. _____ Number the following planets in correct order.

        Mercury   Mars   Saturn   Venus   Jupiter

        _____   _____   _____   _____   _____

2. _____ Congress meets in _____ .

3. _____ Name four rights guaranteed by the constitution and name an instance in which each right has been denied.

4. _____ How many centimeters are there in one meter?

5. _____ The men who wrote the constitution provided different ways to change or amend it. Name two of them.

Items 3 and 4 in this exercise are clearly stated. All of the other items contain faults that make them unclear. In item 1 the basis for ordering the planets is not indicated. Students could arrange the planets according to size, distance from the sun, date of discovery, or alphabetically. Item 2 can be completed with more than one correct answer. Correct answers could include "January," "emergencies," and "Washington, D.C." Item 5 does not clearly indicate what is to be named: two men who wrote the constitution or two ways to amend the constitution.

IDENTIFYING PROMPTED ITEMS

Always try to keep your assessment items free of prompts or clues that students can use to determine correct answers. Items that contain prompts are not likely to provide a valid indication of what students have learned. Some types of prompts that are frequently encountered in teacher-made tests are listed below. Be sure to avoid using prompts such as these.

All right, class, which one is *not* a tropical bird?

• Using specific determiners in true-false items. True-false items that include words such as "always," "never," "only," or "no" are usually false, whereas items that include words such as "frequently," "sometimes," or "may" are usually true.

• Using choices that are obviously incorrect (implausible alternatives) in multiple-choice items. When multiple-choice items contain implausible alternatives, students have a greater chance of selecting the correct alternative because the number of choices to be considered is reduced. The following item is an example.

How many centimeters are there in one meter?
a. 100   c. .001
b. 1.00   d. 3.10

For any student who has studied the metric system, choice d is an implausible alternative. The chance that the student will guess the correct answer to this item is greater because at least one choice can be easily eliminated.

• Using equal numbers of items to be paired in matching items. This type of prompt also increases the chance of a student being able to guess correctly on items not previously learned. Consider the following example.

Match each inventor with his invention.
Joseph Henry   Electric light
Thomas Edison   Electromagnet
Samuel Morse   Electric telegraph

The student who learned only the inventions of Edison and Morse, but not Henry, will nevertheless be able to match Henry with his invention because it will be the only remaining choice. This type of prompt can be avoided by increasing either the number of inventors or the number of inventions listed.

• Including grammatical clues in multiple-choice, completion, and matching items. Articles such as "a" and "an," plural word forms, and gender forms used in multiple-choice items may provide clues to test-wise students that enable them to answer correctly without having learned the content taught.

Exercise 4.4 provides an opportunity to identify whether prompts are present in assessment items. As you read each item, look for the types of prompts just described.

EXERCISE 4.4.   Identifying Prompted Items

Mark an X by each item that is unprompted.

1. _____ Match each element below with its chemical symbol by writing the letter of the symbol in the space provided.

   _____ Gold   a. Hg   d. Fe

   _____ Iron   b. Au   e. Pb

   _____ Lead   c. K   f. I

2. _____ Italy is a
        a. island
        b. isthmus
        c. peninsula

3. _____ A police officer can never search you without a search warrant. (true-false)

4. _____ The legislative branch of government
   a. makes laws
   b. breaks laws
   c. enforces laws

5. _____ Write an original verse that has both the form and the thematic characteristics of haiku.

Items 1 and 5 are unprompted. The number of chemical symbols is larger than the number of elements listed in item 1. Item 5 contains information to indicate the characteristics of an acceptable verse (that is, one with the form and thematic characteristics of haiku), but this information does not constitute a prompt. The other three items contain some form of prompting. Item 2 contains a grammatical prompt: the article "a" in the item limits the correct choice to "peninsula." Item 3 contains a specific determiner, "never," which is more likely to indicate a false statement than a true statement. Item 4 contains an implausible choice, "breaks laws."

Prompting is not limited to written assessment materials. You can also prompt student performance by your actions when administering a test. Nodding approval, looking at objects to be manipulated, and silently mouthing responses may prompt students. You should also avoid an unusually high frequency of placing a correct choice in the same position among several choices.

Exercise 4.5 requires you to determine whether assessment items are well written. Read each item both for clarity and for prompting.

EXERCISE 4.5.   Identifying Well-Written Items

Mark an X by each well-written assessment item.

1. _____ Tuberculosis is caused by a
   a. fungus
   b. bacillus
   c. virus

2. _____ List the following names in alphabetical order:

   Abraham, Abel, Alabama, Aaron, Ableman.

3. _____ Describe one procedure for amending the U.S. Constitution.

4. _____ List some of the constitutional qualifications for the U.S. presidency.

5. _____ Match the prefixes with their meanings by writing the letter of the meaning in the space provided.

   _____ Pre   a. across or over

   _____ Post   b. before

   _____ Trans   c. after

You should have marked items 1, 2, and 3. They are well-written assessment items. The others are not. Item 4 is not clearly stated, because the number of qualifications to be listed is ambiguous. Item 5 contains a prompt (equal number of items in both lists) that increases the student's chance of answering correctly.

WRITING ASSESSMENT ITEMS

Writing assessment items for instructional objectives is a straight-forward matter. The items for an objective must (1) require the student to perform the exact task specified in the objective and (2) contain the conditions or givens, if any, specified in the objective. The item must also be clearly written and free of prompts. Some common types of test performances, as stated in objectives, and considerations for assessing them follow.

IDENTIFYING

Assessment items directly reflect the performance stated in an instructional objective. In assessment of student learning, we often ask students to *identify* examples of concepts and principles, appropriate attitudes, or correct ways of doing tasks. Instructional objectives that specify performances such as *select* or *distinguish between* require assessment items that call for the student to pick out (that is, identify) correct answers. Items written to assess performance on these objectives must include examples and non-examples of the things to be identified and directions for how to indicate the examples. Consider an item for assessing the following objective.

The student will identify the peninsulas on an outline map.

What kinds of examples and non-examples would you include in the assessment item? How could students indicate the examples? The assessment item should include an outline map (the given in the objective) that contains examples and non-examples of peninsulas (isthmuses, islands, or capes). Obviously, the item must also include directions that indicate how the student is to identify the examples of peninsulas on the map. Directions such as "Point to the peninsulas" and "Mark the peninsulas with an *X*" indicate how the student is to identify the examples.

If the objective requires the student to identify examples of two or more types of things, the examples for one type can serve as non-examples for the other type(s). An elementary science objective specifies that students will identify objects made of wood, of plastic, and of metal. When performance of this objective is assessed, the student is given objects made of wood (such as dowels and blocks) and similar objects made of plastic and metal. Objects that are examples of wood will also serve as non-examples for plastic and metal.

Exercise 4.6 provides practice in writing test items in which students identify correct answers. Remember to include (1) both examples and plausible non-examples of the things to be identified and (2) clear directions for how to indicate the examples.

EXERCISE 4.6.   Writing Assessment Items

Write an item that would assess performance on the following objective.

Objective: The student will identify the squares, given examples of squares and other four-sided figures.

Assessment item:

There are several ways to assess performance on this objective. Your answer is correct if it includes (1) a set of four-sided figures, some of which are squares, and (2) directions for how to indicate the squares. Following is a sample item for assessing this objective.

Assessment item: Check (✓) the squares.

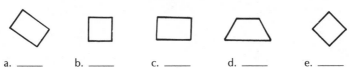

a. _____   b. _____   c. _____   d. _____   e. _____

The sample item presents a situation in which five four-sided figures are given. The student identifies the examples of squares by checking (✓) them.

NAMING

Another task that students are often asked to perform is to give the names for objects, processes, concepts, or principles. Objectives that specify performances such as *label* and *list* involve naming something from memory. It is important to determine whether the names are to be associated with specific objects, listed in a particular order, or simply listed in any order. Consider the following objectives that involve naming performances:

Label the lens, iris, retina, and optic nerve on a longitudinal-section illustration of the eye.

List the major geologic eras from earliest to most recent.

Name the three branches of the federal government.

The assessment for the first objective requires associating names with specific illustrated objects (parts of the eye) and should include a longitudinal-section drawing of the eye. The parts of the eye to be named would be indicated on the illustration, and the directions would require the student to write the name for each part indicated.

The assessment items for the second and third objectives would simply be restatements of the instructional objectives. Unlike the first objective, they do not require associating the names with specific objects or illustrations. For the second objective, the geologic eras must be named in a specific order (earliest to most recent). For the third, the student must name the branches of government, but not in a particular order.

Complete exercise 4.7 in writing assessment items for objectives that require the students to supply the answers by naming them from memory. Do not include the names that the students must supply. Otherwise, they would not have to provide the names from memory.

EXERCISE 4.7.   Writing Assessment Items

Write assessment items for the following objectives.

1. *Objective*: The student will label the crown and root areas on an illustration of a tooth.

   Assessment item:

2. *Objective*: The student will name the saws used in wood shop, when shown actual saws of each type. (Note: the saws are rip, crosscut, keyhole, and coping.)

Assessment item:

The assessment for the first objective should include either an illustration of a tooth with the crown and the root areas indicated, but not named, or a statement specifying that such an illustration would be included. The directions should require the student to label (or name) each area. A correct example is shown below.

Assessment item: Name the parts of the tooth pictured below.

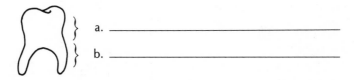

The directions for the second item should require the student to either write or say the name of each saw. The saws can be shown individually by the teacher or they can be displayed as a group. Two sample assessment items that would be correct for this objective are listed here.

Assessment item: Write the name of each saw as it is shown.

1. _____ 2. _____ 3. _____ 4. _____

Assessment item: Each of the four saws on the workbench has a letter painted on it. Write the name of each saw by its letter below.

a. _____ c. _____

b. _____ d. _____

Answers similar to these may also be counted as correct.

COMPLEX PERFORMANCES

Many of the things students are expected to learn are much more complex than identifying and naming. Some examples of objectives that require complex performances are *Describe a painting, Operate a slide projector, Skip rope,* and *Make a leather key case.* Some complex performances must be assessed at the time and place they occur. Others result in products that can be assessed without directly observing the performance. Operating a slide projector and skipping rope are examples of the former. A description of a painting and a leather key case are products that may be examined after their production to determine if students have learned the desired skills.

The assessment for an objective requiring a complex performance or a student product involves (1) directing the student to perform the tasks stated in the objective, (2) providing the givens, if any, and (3) checking the student's performance or product against specified criteria. The task the student is to perform and the givens are included in the objective. The criteria used to assess the performance or product must be set by the teacher. They may simply be listed or kept in mind by the teacher.

The criteria used to assess complex performances should be limited to the important characteristics of the performance or product. It is preferable to set criteria that can be checked on an "all-or-nothing" basis rather than rated on a continuous scale. Following is an example that illustrates criteria for assessing complex performances.

Objective: The student will do two forward rolls (somersaults) in succession.

If you were assessing this objective, you would tell the students to do two forward rolls and would check each student's performance using specific assessment criteria. The criteria might include the following items.

- Uses proper form for each roll
- Completes two rolls in a continuous motion
- Stays on the tumbling mat

After you checked the student's performance against the criteria, scores could be derived for the performance in either of two ways. You could assign a number score based on one point for each of the criteria demonstrated (0–3), or you could assign a pass or fail grade based on whether the student met a predetermined number of the criteria (e.g., all three criteria or two out of three).

Following is an example that involves the assessment of a product.

Objective: The student will write an original verse that has the form and the thematic characteristics of haiku.

When assessing this objective, you would direct the student to write an original haiku. The finished verse would be assessed using specific criteria such as those which follow.

- Writes an original verse
- Uses three lines with 5-7-5 syllable pattern
- States or implies a relationship between two seemingly unrelated things

The three criteria relate to the characteristics specified in the instructional objective (originality, form, and theme). As with the previous example, you could score the verse on the number of criteria demonstrated or on a pass-fail basis.

In both of the previous examples, the criteria listed were limited to important characteristics of the performances or products being assessed. Exercises 4.8 and 4.9 provide an opportunity to practice writing assessment items for complex performances.

EXERCISE 4.8. Writing Assessment Items

Write the directions to the student and the criteria that would be used to assess student performance on the following objective.

Objective: Given the text of the speech, the student will deliver a persuasive speech using appropriate public speaking techniques.

Directions:

Criteria:

The directions should indicate that the student is to deliver a persuasive speech from a given text. They might also indicate that the speech will be assessed on public speaking techniques that had been taught. Following are criteria commonly used to assess public speaking.

- Maintains good posture
- Maintains eye contact with audience
- Speaks loudly enough to be heard by all
- Speaks slowly and clearly enough to be understood
- Uses appropriate gestures

Your assessment criteria should not relate to the contents of the speech, since the text of the speech was provided for the student.

Exercise 4.9. Writing Assessment Items

Write the directions to the student and the criteria that would be used to assess performance on the following objective.

Objective: Given a job announcement, the student will write a letter of application for the job.

Directions:

Criteria:

Your directions should require the student to write a letter of application for a job. Some criteria that could be used for assessing letters of application are listed here.

- Indicates job being applied for
- States qualifications for the job
- Requests an interview to discuss the job
- Uses proper business letter form
- Contains no grammatical or spelling errors
- Is neatly written or typed

Again, it is possible to have other criteria that you feel are important for assessing the quality of the letter.

ATTITUDE-RELATED PERFORMANCES

You can best assess attitude-related objectives in real-life situations in which the attitudes or interests are expected to occur. You must obtain a record of student performance in these situations, either by observing it directly or by having students report their own behavior. You can often determine on your own whether students display the desired behaviors for attitudes or interests that are manifested at school. These include reading during free time, participation in school activities, compliance with conduct rules, and completion of optional assignments. For attitude-related behaviors that occur away from school (reading for pleasure, attending cultural events, or performing community service), it may be necessary for you to rely on student reports of their own behavior. Though such reports are sometimes unreliable, they may be your best source of assessment information for away-from-school activities.

In some situations either it is not feasible to use behavior to indicate student attitudes or it is desirable to have attitudinal information in addition to direct observation of behavior. Attitude questionnaires or surveys are appropriate for use in these situations. For example, suppose you wanted your students to have a positive attitude toward school. You could use direct measures of behavior, such as attendance records and performance in submitting class assignments, to assess this attitude. An additional measure that might be a good indicator of the attitude would be a questionnaire on attitudes toward school.

Procedures for constructing attitude questionnaires or surveys are not covered in this book. They can be found in any current book on attitude assessment.

CONCLUSION

Chapter 4 has dealt with several basic considerations in developing competency-based assessment procedures. You have learned to identify appropriate assessment items for given instructional objectives, to identify well-written items, and to write good assessment items for instructional objectives. These skills provide you with a good foundation for constructing assessment items and tests for use in your own teaching. They will also help you to determine how effective your teaching is and how much your students learn from it.

Now try the self test for Chapter 4 on pages 96–98.

ADDITIONAL LEARNING ACTIVITIES

1. Select a set of instructional objectives for a unit of instruction. Prepare materials for assessing student attainment of the objectives. If possible, compare the assessment materials you developed with those prepared by others. Discuss the similarities and differences in the assessment materials.

TABLE 1

Name	Pretest-Posttest Percentage Scores							
	A		B		C		D	
Angel	90	90	70	75	40	50	30	50
Bonnie	100	100	60	100	50	90	50	90
Donald	90	95	70	85	30	65	10	40
Jose	80	85	50	90	45	50	30	50
Marta	90	100	70	80	40	45	20	50
Nancy	60	65	40	50	30	40	10	20
Patrick	65	80	45	50	30	45	0	20
Sam	90	100	50	95	35	55	30	40
Tanya	85	95	55	85	30	60	20	50
William	100	100	70	100	60	90	40	90
Average (Mean)	85	91	58	81	39	59	24	50

2. Teachers may have difficulty reconciling the high levels of student performance sometimes attained on objectives-based tests with traditional grading systems. Discuss (1) how grades are used in school settings and (2) ways of converting student scores on objectives-based tests to letter grades.

3. Test scores for 10 students on four objectives of an eighth-grade nutrition unit are given in table 1. Discuss with others how these test scores might be used to determine which objectives have been attained, to identify students who need remediation, and to determine objectives for which instruction should be revised.

OBJECTIVES

A. Classify foods into four food groups.
B. Identify the number of servings in specified foods.
C. Name the number of servings needed from each food group.
D. Prepare a one-day menu from a given diet plan.

Chapter 5

MAKING
CBI WORK

By now you know a lot about CBI. You've learned to write worthwhile objectives, to design effective instruction, and to prepare good assessment items. But suppose that you were going to start teaching a new course soon and you wanted to use CBI techniques to do it. How would you go about it? That's what this final chapter is about.

Remember the dialogue between the authors about whether you should just *think about* your instruction in the CBI manner *or* actually *do* it that way? Well, one perfectly acceptable way to use CBI in teaching your course is just to think through the course CBI style as you go along. Let your thinking and the principles of CBI guide your instruction, but do not try to prepare all the CBI-related materials in written form. We have referred to this process as just thinking about your course in the CBI manner, but it really involves more than that. You do, in fact, consistently apply CBI principles in planning and delivering your instruction. This CBI approach to instruction takes no more preparation time than other teaching methods, and doing it conscientiously will ensure that your course is well taught.

A more complete and structured process, but also a more time-consuming one, is to prepare the major CBI components of your course (sets of objectives, supplementary instructional materials, and end-of-unit tests) in written form. Naturally, this is necessary if, either individually or with a group, you are developing a course for other teachers as well as yourself. Once the materials are well prepared, the course should be very effective and relatively easy to teach. However, you may feel that this process takes more time than you can afford for most courses. In that case, you may decide to develop complete CBI materials in written form for a course only over a period of years or in the subject-matter areas that you feel are most important.

This chapter is organized around three topics: developing a CBI course, instructing in a CBI course, and improving your instruction. It is intended as a "how to do it" guide for using CBI to plan and teach your own courses. After you have read it, you can use it as a reference at any future time that you are involved in these processes.

DEVELOPING A CBI COURSE

Under normal conditions you are likely to develop most of the CBI-related materials for a course as you go along during the school year. You can let the amount of time that you have available help you determine the degree to which you prepare materials in written form, as contrasted with just thinking through the course CBI style. Either way, you use the basic procedures summarized here.

1. Determine the course content.
2. Divide the content into units.
3. Determine the objectives for Unit 1.
4. Select or prepare the instruction for the unit.
5. Prepare the unit assessment.
6. Repeat steps 3 through 5 for each succeeding unit.

Notice that the objectives-instruction-assessment cycle that was the basis for Chapters 2 through 4 shows up again as steps 3 through 5 in this list.

Following is a description of what to do for each of the six steps in developing a course.

1. *Determine the course content.* Your first step is to select the content that you think should be taught in the course. At this stage, the content should still be at a general level. You should identify broad topics, chapters, major themes, or performances that constitute large chunks of important content for your students. Write them down, even if you're using the "think through" process, because you'll need to refer to them later. Then sequence them so that you are sure that you will have time to complete the most important segments during the course and so that basic or prerequisite skills are taught prior to more comprehensive skills that depend on mastery of the basics.

The textbook that you choose or are assigned to use for the course will normally be your best single source for identifying content. But beware of going straight through the book without either judging the worth of its content or supplementing it with other content. Additional sources that can help you identify good content include other textbooks, school district or state curriculum guides, and your own ideas and those of other teachers.

2. *Divide the content into units.* The idea here is to break up the course into a schedule that will enable you to cover all of the planned content and that provides for regular assessment of student progress. Insofar as possible, a unit should consist of a related body of content or set of skills. For this step you should take your content groupings and organize them into units. Decide what you think is a reasonable length of time to complete each unit and allocate that amount to it. For each unit just briefly note the major content to be covered and the approximate amount of time. The total length of time for all units should be approximately equal to the time available for the course. Add or subtract content as appropriate to get the desired course length, but don't worry too much about how accurate your time estimates are. It may be necessary to adjust them later when you work with the units on a more detailed basis.

In allocating time to each unit of instruction, you should keep in mind that the end of a unit typically is the best time to assess student learning. Assessment at this point enables you to detect and, if necessary, remediate deficiencies in the learning of individual students or the entire class before they fall too far behind. Thus, a unit should not be so long that specific learning problems can go undetected until they become a serious handicap. How long is this? Well, it may vary a great deal depending on grade level and subject matter. For first graders who are learning many new basic reading skills and who may have relatively short memory spans, a suitable unit length might be two to three weeks. For high school or college students studying more general content in a survey-type course, unit lengths and between-testing periods could conceivably be much longer.

As a general rule, you should try to divide the units in a course so that they are approximately equal in duration and/or include approximately equal amounts of content to be learned. Of course, the nature of the subject matter in some fields is such that you may not always be able to do this.

3. *Determine the objectives for Unit 1.* For this step you examine your general content and available instructional materials for the first unit and derive specific instructional objectives from them. What are

the important things students should learn to do in this unit? These become your unit objectives.

This is a crucial step. Give a lot of thought to it. Don't include everything in your textbook as an objective just because it's there. Instead, apply what you learned in the earlier chapter on worthwhile objectives to derive skills that you think are really important for your students to learn. Eliminate those that you judge to be not worthwhile and any other content that you feel is not valuable. Add objectives other than those in your text if you think they are important and if they fall within your curriculum scope and grade level. In order to help with scheduling and sequencing, try to determine your objectives for a unit before beginning instruction for it.

Normally you should not include more than a few objectives in a single unit. In fact, there may be only one if it involves a very complex performance. On the other hand, there may be up to five or more if you are teaching several less complex skills. Write down each objective in very brief form (once you have decided on the objectives, it will only take a minute or two for a unit), or at least keep each one firmly in mind as you plan and deliver the instruction for it. After all, these objectives will be the cornerstones of your instructional program.

4. *Select or prepare the instruction for the unit.* You are now ready to select and/or prepare the instructional materials and procedures for each objective in the unit. Often this will be easiest to do on an objective-by-objective basis as you are teaching the unit. Remember, you want your students to get the necessary information, the appropriate type and amount of direct practice, and the desired feedback for each objective. You are almost certain to find that the textbook does not always supply these essentials exactly as needed for your class. If it doesn't, decide how you can supplement it. Can you do it adequately the easier way—with information, practice, and feedback in oral form only? Or are written exercises or assignments needed? Do as much as you can to provide the most desirable instruction. You may find that time does not permit you to do everything you'd like the first time you teach a course, but you should be able to get a good start that you can continue to build on in the future.

5. *Prepare the unit assessment.* This step involves preparing the materials to assess student performance on the instructional objectives for the unit. The items for each objective should have the characteristics of good assessment items as described in Chapter 4. You simply write

items as you did for the objectives in the last few exercises in that chapter.

Unit assessment can range from simple to complex at the teacher's discretion. A simple form is to measure performance only on the major skill or skills, but not the subskills, included in the unit. For example, suppose that you were constructing a test over Chapter 4, Assessment, in this book. The final objective for the chapter is "The student will write good assessment items for instructional objectives." This is the most important objective for the chapter and it subsumes the other two objectives—identifying appropriate assessment items and identifying well-written items. You could formally assess performance only on this final objective because it is the major skill for the chapter. You would include several items for this one objective so that you would have a good measure of each student's overall ability on it.

A more complex form of unit assessment is to measure performance on each objective for the unit, rather than just on the major skill or skills. Again, you should include several items—say, three or more—for every objective that involves a relatively simple performance such as an identifying or naming response. Then you organize the items into a test with the ones for each individual objective grouped together. This form of assessment will take you more time than assessing performance on major skills only, but it yields more precise information about student learning.

A single item may be used for unit assessment on objectives requiring a complex performance. The item should have a maximum possible score of several points, so that it counts more than the individual items on objectives involving simple responses. The complex performance or product need not be produced in a normal testing situation. For example, the unit assessment for a particular objective could consist of an essay or drawing done either in class or outside.

The self tests for Chapters 2, 3, and 4 in the appendices of this book are examples of one form of unit test. They are shorter than the unit tests that the authors use when teaching a CBI course, but they give you an idea of what a rather complete unit test looks like. You can see that the tests are organized into parts that assess one objective each and that a total test covers all objectives for its chapter.

There is one other thing that you should have with your unit test. That's a form on which you record each student's score for each objective that is assessed and for the total test. You will probably find it most convenient to use a standard class record book for this purpose, although you can construct a separate record form that is referenced directly to your objectives on a unit-by-unit basis. The self test record form in Appendix A of this book is an example of such a record form for an individual student.

6. *Repeat steps 3 through 5 for each succeeding unit.* At this point you will have finished everything for Unit 1. As you continue with the course, repeat the process for each new unit. The first unit is usually the most difficult because you're doing everything for the first time. The things you learn in doing it will make the other units easier.

By way of review, let's look at what you'll have when you're finished with the course:

- A unit-by-unit schedule and listing of the major course content
- A set of worthwhile objectives for each unit
- Instructional materials and procedures for each objective
- The assessment for each unit
- A form for recording student progress through the course

INSTRUCTING IN A CBI COURSE

Doing the actual instruction is the process that keeps you busy in the classroom. You already have learned the key principles of instruction as they relate to individual objectives. That was the focus of Chapter 3. There are just a few additional things to consider when you are teaching an entire unit.

One consideration is introducing the unit. When you begin a new unit, you should introduce it in much the same way that you introduce a new learning activity. Preview the unit for the students. Tell them the objectives in easily understood language and inform them of the types of activities they will be participating in. Explain the importance of what they will be learning. Do your best to motivate them for the unit and to stimulate their interest in it.

Delivering the instruction for the unit is, of course, the heart of the CBI process. Here you will be working with the materials that you have selected or prepared for your unit objectives. For each objective, follow the procedures that you learned in Chapter 3 so that you provide your students with appropriate information, practice, and feedback. Take care to see that your students can perform well on each objective in the unit before going on to the next one, even if it means adding a new activity or two for unexpectedly difficult objectives. Try to make each activity as enjoyable as possible for the students.

When you've completed the instruction for the unit, your students should be well prepared for the assessment. It is a good idea to review the unit content with the students a day or two before testing them. Don't feel that the test should surprise or deceive them in any way. It should simply be a straightforward, unbiased assessment of their performance on the unit objectives, and they should understand that fact. You want them to do well on it. That is the best sign that they have mastered the objectives and that you did a good job of teaching. After you have administered the test, score it and record each student's score. If the test assessed performance on several objectives, record scores both for each objective and for the total test. Then review the test with the class, providing feedback in the manner described in Chapter 3. Have the students look at their own tests during the review so that they can see and learn from their right and wrong answers.

You've introduced the unit, delivered the instruction for it, and administered and reviewed the unit test. Is there anything else for you to do before going on to the next unit? One option to consider is to provide remediation at this time. Suppose that the scores on your test record form show that the class in general had low achievement on one or two objectives or that several students did poorly on the entire test. This is the best time for you to present additional instruction. You can provide this remediation as needed, for either the entire class or just certain individuals on the objectives on which performance was low. Review the difficult content and give the students concentrated practice on it so that they can improve their performance before moving on to a new unit.

IMPROVING YOUR INSTRUCTION

Now imagine that you have taught the entire course once. You have recorded students' scores on each test. It is easy to convert these scores to percentages so that you can see the average percentage score for your class on the tests and on individual objectives and the total test. What level of performance are you willing to accept? Seventy percent? Eighty percent? Some other figure? The answer will undoubtedly depend on such factors as the difficulty of the particular test or objectives and the ability level of your class. Still, one thing is certain. You will have a good indication of where the students have done well and where they haven't. You will know where to concentrate your efforts at course improvement. The second time you teach the course you can focus on improving it, rather than on the course development that occupied you the first time through.

Knowing where the achievement problems are in your course is one step toward improving it, but knowing what to do about these problems can still be tough to figure out. Try your own ideas first. See if you can think of changes that are likely to work in the problem areas. Talk to other teachers too if you think they can help. And don't forget the students themselves if they are old enough to be a good source of information. If students don't learn something that you teach, they can often tell you what the problem is. Don't wait until the end of the course to ask them. Do it at the end of the relevant unit or as soon as the problem becomes evident.

One good bet for improving achievement in areas where students have not performed well is simply to add more basic instruction. Present and review the instructional information in its simplest form. Increase the amount of individual practice and the number and variety of appropriate learning activities. Give the students feedback on their performance as they go along and not just at the end of an activity. Concentrated instruction of this type is almost sure to work well.

In a CBI course, the process of improving your instruction can be very challenging to you as a teacher. You will often have concrete evidence that your students are doing well in most areas, but you will know that

there is a need for improvement in a few others. These areas become the focus of your course improvement efforts. You try out new ideas and materials in an attempt to bring about the desired improvements. When your ideas and materials work, the results are very rewarding.

CONCLUSION

In this book we have covered the points you need to know about competency-based instruction to use it successfully in the classroom. You have learned how to decide what your students should learn, how to teach it well, and how to tell whether the students have learned it. You now know how to do these things both on a day-to-day basis and for an entire course.

CBI can help you become an excellent teacher. Here are some reasons why.

1. *It's effective.* Your students will learn quickly and well.
2. *It's student-centered.* The focus is on the things that are important for *students* to learn, on *student* participation and practice, and on checking to see that *students* are doing well.
3. *It's individualized.* It features a high rate of *individual* practice for all students and an *individualized* basis for providing remediation to only those students who need it.
4. *It's rewarding.* Your achievement and that of your students will be obvious in their performance. Both you and the students will have a strong sense of personal accomplishment.

As you can tell, we think CBI is a fine teaching method. We use it with our own classes and we followed CBI principles in developing this book. Now that you are well prepared in CBI, we hope that you too will use it in your teaching.

ADDITIONAL LEARNING ACTIVITIES

1. As mentioned in Developing a CBI Course in this chapter, you would have the following components after developing your own CBI course.
   • A unit-by-unit schedule and listing of the major course content
   • A set of worthwhile objectives for each unit
   • The instructional materials and procedures for each objective
   • The assessment for each unit
   • A form for recording student progress through the course

Choose a teacher's guide for a course and any other materials that are designed to be used with it. Do the following:

a. Determine which of the above components are included in the guide and accompanying materials.

b. Analyze how adequate each included component is for its purpose.

c. Determine what, if anything, would be needed to make the materials work well in a CBI course.

2. Individually or with others prepare a short unit of instruction for a course in any subject area to be taught using CBI. Use any existing instructional materials that are available to you and supplement them as needed. Be sure to include at least the instructional objectives for the unit, the instructional materials, and the unit test.

3. The preparation of this book and its prepublication field testing by 10 instructors with more than 400 preservice and inservice teachers are described in the following short article.

Higgins, N., and Sullivan, H. Preparing Special Education Teachers for Competency-Based Instruction. *Teacher Education and Special Education*, 1983, 5(4).

Read this article and discuss it with others. Note especially the reasons for the content of the book and how well students learned from it in the field test. You will notice that the article emphasizes special education. That is because there was a high proportion of special education teachers in several tryout classes, and therefore the article was written for a special education journal. However, as the article notes, both it and the book itself are equally appropriate for regular education classes.

APPENDICES
INDEX

Appendix A

SELF TEST
RECORD FORM

The 13 skills taught in Chapters 2, 3, and 4 are listed below. The number of items that assess each objective on the self tests in Appendices B–D is given after the objective. You can record the number of self test items you answered correctly in the space provided.

	TOTAL POSSIBLE	YOUR SCORE

CHAPTER 2, WORTHWHILE OBJECTIVES

1. Distinguishing objectives from activities: items 1–4 — 4 ☐

2. Identifying worthwhile objectives: items 5–8 — 4 ☐

3. Identifying well-written objectives: items 9–12 — 4 ☐

4. Writing instructional objectives: items 13–14 — 2 ☐

   Total — 14 ☐

CHAPTER 3, EFFECTIVE INSTRUCTION

5. Identifying appropriate information: items 1–3 — 3 ☐

6. Providing information: items 4–5 — 2 ☐

7. Identifying appropriate practice: items 6–8 — 3 ☐

8. Providing appropriate practice: items 9–10 — 2 ☐

9. Identifying effective practice activities: items 11–13 — 3 ☐

10. Identifying effective feedback activities: items 14–16 — 3 ☐

   Total — 16 ☐

CHAPTER 4, ASSESSMENT

	TOTAL POSSIBLE	YOUR SCORE
11. Identifying appropriate assessment items: items 1–4	4	☐
12. Identifying well-written items: items 5–8	4	☐
13. Writing assessment items: items 9–11	3	☐
Total	11	☐

SELF TEST FOR CHAPTER 2, WORTHWHILE OBJECTIVES

Directions: Answer each item below. Complete the entire test before checking your answers.

PART 1. DISTINGUISHING OBJECTIVES FROM ACTIVITIES

Write an *O* by each instructional objective and an *A* by each activity.

1. _____ The student will visit a community service agency on a class field trip.

2. _____ The student will write an original ballad.

3. _____ The student will rehearse a speech, using a prepared copy of the speech.

4. _____ The student will name the primary colors, when shown examples of each color.

PART 2. IDENTIFYING WORTHWHILE OBJECTIVES

Mark an *X* by the more worthwhile objective in each pair of objectives.

5a. _____ Given a map with a scale of 1 inch to 100 miles, the student will describe how to figure the distance between two points on the map.

5b. _____ Given a map with a scale of 1 inch to 100 miles and the names of five pairs of cities on the map, the student will figure the direct distance between each pair to the nearest 100 miles.

6a. _____ The student will attend at least two out-of-school plays during the school year.

6b. _____ The student will demonstrate a positive attitude toward drama by rating drama activities favorably on a standardized interest survey.

7a. _____ The student will name the constitutional rights guaranteed by the Bill of Rights.

7b. _____ Given descriptions of instances in which constitutional rights have been invoked or denied, the student will name the rights involved.

8a. _____ The student will spell the new spelling words correctly when they are given orally.

8b. _____ The student will identify each correctly spelled word, given a list of the new spelling words with each word spelled both correctly and incorrectly.

Part 3. Identifying Well-Written Objectives

Mark an X by each objective that is well written.

9. _____ Given multiple-choice questions showing causes and non-causes of dietary diseases, the student will identify the causes.

10. _____ The student will describe the similarities of and the differences between a square and a rectangle.

11. _____ The student will learn the characteristics of free enterprise as described in the class text.

12. _____ The student will be shown the proper way to sew a buttonhole.

Part 4. Writing Instructional Objectives

13. Write an instructional objective for teaching the concepts "left" and "right."
Objective:

14. Write an instructional objective that indicates students will have a positive attitude toward science and that does not involve use of an attitude scale.
    Objective:

After completing the entire self test, check your answers against the answer key that follows.

ANSWER KEY

PART 1	PART 2
1. *A*	5. b
2. *O*	6. a
3. *A*	7. b
4. *O*	8. a

PART 3

9. Not well written (the givens are stated incorrectly).
10. Well written.
11. Not well written (the verb "learn" does not describe an observable performance).
12. Not well written (the student performance is not described).

PART 4

13. Score your objective as correct if it (a) specifies an observable student performance for the concepts "left" and "right" and (b) indicates the givens. Examples of correct answers include:

    Given sets of two or more objects, the student will identify the object on the right and the object on the left.

    The student will identify right and left parts of his or her body as directed by the teacher.

    As noted in (a), you should also consider your objective correct if it specifies an observable student performance for "left" and "right" and indicates the givens.
14. Score your objective as correct if it specifies a voluntary and observable student performance that indicates a positive attitude toward science. Examples of correct answers include:

    The student will watch an average of at least two nonfiction science programs a month on television during the school year.

    The student will voluntarily perform at least one of the following activities during the year: enter the science fair, visit a science museum, attend a science lecture, or read one or more nonfiction science books.

Now record your scores on the self test record form in Appendix A.

If you missed one or more items on any part of the self test, you may find it helpful to reread the material related to that part of the test. Review of the relevant section of the text is especially important if you missed a test item and you do not understand why your answer was incorrect after you have read the answers given above.

SELF TEST FOR CHAPTER 3, EFFECTIVE INSTRUCTION

Directions: Answer each item below. Complete the entire test before checking your answers.

PART 1. IDENTIFYING INSTRUCTIONAL INFORMATION

Mark an X if the information is appropriate for enabling students to perform the task stated in the objective. Mark an O if the information is not appropriate.

1. _____ *Objective*: The student will use appropriate table manners when eating classroom snacks.
Information: If you don't use good table manners, we won't have any more snacks in class.

2. _____ *Objective*: Given the weight of an object and the distance it is to be moved, the student will compute the work required to move the object.
Information: To determine the work required to move an object, multiply its weight by the distance it is to be moved.

3. _____ *Objective*: The student will name the letter *c* when it is presented in lower case.
Information: This is the letter *c*. . . . (Show the letter *c*.) . . . Say "*c*."

PART 2. PROVIDING INFORMATION

Write the information you would provide to enable students to perform each of the following objectives.

4. *Objective*: When shown the letters *b* and *d*, the student will say the sound for each letter.

Information:

5. *Objective*: The student will reduce fractions with one-digit denominators to their lowest terms. (Example: $6/9 = 2/3$)
   Information:

PART 3. IDENTIFYING APPROPRIATE PRACTICE

Mark an *X* if the activity provides appropriate practice for the objective. Mark an *O* if the practice is not appropriate.

6. _____ *Objective*: The student will name the natural regions (desert, grassland, forest, or tundra) represented in pictures of those regions.
   Practice: Give each student a picture of a natural region. Have each student state the natural features present in his or her picture until other students can guess the name of the region pictured.

7. _____ *Objective*: The student will prepare an outline for a persuasive speech.
   Practice: Give the students two or three outlines for persuasive speeches. Have them select the best outline and discuss the characteristics of that outline.

8. _____ *Objective*: The student will say the names of the primary and secondary colors in Spanish when given examples of each color.
   Practice: Give each student a color wheel painted with the primary and secondary colors. Have each student spin the wheel and state the Spanish word for the color that comes up on top of the wheel each time.

PART 4. PROVIDING APPROPRIATE PRACTICE

Describe an activity that would provide appropriate practice for the following objectives.

9. *Objective:* The student will use a dictionary to pronounce words which cannot be sounded out (for example, pneumonia, partial).
   Practice:

10. *Objective:* Given the cost and the quantities of various canned foods, the student will identify the most economical buy for each food.
    Practice:

PART 5. IDENTIFYING INDIVIDUAL AND FREQUENT PRACTICE

Mark an *X* by the correct choice for each of the following items.

11. Which activity would provide the most frequent practice for the objective "The student will read aloud in a fluent manner"?

   a. _____ Have the students turn to a story in their readers; then call on individual students in a random manner to read a paragraph aloud.

   b. _____ Divide the students into groups of three and have the students in each group take turns reading paragraphs aloud from a story in their readers.

   c. _____ Have one student read aloud until he or she makes an error. Let the student who caught the error read until he or she makes an error. Continue the procedure until the story is completed.

12. Which activity would provide the best practice for the objective "The student will perform two forward rolls in succession"?

   a. _____ Select those students with poor motor coordination and have them do forward rolls while the students with good coordination provide encouragement.

   b. _____ Have all students do forward rolls during the practice period.

   c. _____ Call on volunteers to do forward rolls to avoid embarrassing students who may not be able to perform adequately.

13. Which procedure would be best for calling on students during an oral practice activity?

    a. _____ Call on individual students in the order listed in the class book to ensure that every student is called on.

    b. _____ Call on the entire class to respond together, thus giving all students an equal opportunity to respond.

    c. _____ Call on individual students in a random manner, being sure that all students respond an equal number of times.

PART 6. PROVIDING KNOWLEDGE OF RESULTS

Mark an X by the correct choice for each of the following items.

14. Beth is called on to say the Spanish word for "green." She is hesitant in making her response. Which comment provides the best way to prompt her?

    a. _____ "Is it 'verde' or 'azul'?"

    b. _____ "There is a tree called a paloverde tree. Does that help you?"

    c. _____ "It starts with the letter v, Beth."

15. Kelly is asked to state three characteristics of mammals. He names two characteristics but cannot remember the third. Which comment provides the best feedback in this situation?

    a. _____ "Kelly, you have only given two characteristics. Who can tell Kelly what the third characteristic is?"

    b. _____ "You named two characteristics, Kelly. The third characteristic is that mammals are warm blooded. Now state all three characteristics."

    c. _____ "Think hard, Kelly. Two out of three is good. Now how does a dog differ from a fish?"

16. Students have submitted written essays which present pro and con arguments on controversial issues. Which is the best procedure for providing feedback on their essays?

    a. _____ Mark the pro and con statements for correctness. Return the papers to the students and review common errors. Have the students who have errors correct them.

    b. _____ Mark all of the errors on the paper, including errors in grammar and spelling. Return the papers to the students.

    c. _____ Mark the pro and con statements for correctness. Return the papers to the students. Post the copies of the best essays on the bulletin board.

ANSWER KEY

PART 1

1. *O* (Statement does not tell student what appropriate table manners are.)
2. *X*
3. *X*

PART 2

4. Score your information correct if it tells the student the sounds for the letters *b* and *d*. An example of the correct information is given below.

> The sound for this letter (show *b*) is "buh." The sound for this letter (show *d*) is "duh."

5. Score your information correct if it tells the student how to reduce a fraction to its lowest terms. Two examples of correct information are given here.

> Find a number that will divide evenly (no remainder) into both the numerator and the denominator of the fraction. Divide the numerator and denominator by this number. Continue until there is no number that will divide evenly into the numerator and denominator.

> Divide both the numerator and the denominator by the largest number that will go into them without leaving a remainder.

PART 3

6. *O* (The activity does not provide appropriate "givens.")
7. *O* (The activity does not require an appropriate student performance.)
8. *X*

PART 4

9. An appropriate activity for this objective would involve (a) giving each student a dictionary and a list of words and (b) telling students to look up each word in the dictionary and practice pronouncing it.

Score your activity correct if it provides appropriate givens and requires student practice in pronouncing the word.

10. An appropriate activity should indicate how the costs and quantities of canned foods will be given and how students will identify the most economical buy. An example of an appropriate activity is described below.

Use the overhead projector to present a list of canned food prices and quantities. Have the students write the letter or brand of the foods that are the most economical.

PART 5	PART 6
11. b	14. a
12. b	15. b
13. c	16. a

Now record your scores on the self test record form in Appendix A.

If you missed one or more items on any part of the self test, you may find it helpful to reread the material related to that part of the test. Review of the relevant section of the text is especially important if you missed a test item and you do not understand why your answer was incorrect after you have read the answers given above.

SELF TEST FOR
CHAPTER 4, ASSESSMENT

Directions: Answer each item below. Complete the entire test before checking your answers.

PART 1. IDENTIFYING APPROPRIATE ASSESSMENT ITEMS

Mark an X if the item is appropriate for assessing the objective. Mark an O if the item is not appropriate.

1. _____ *Objective*: The student will demonstrate appropriate procedures for leaving the school building during fire drill.
   Assessment: You will be shown six slides of students leaving the building during a fire drill. Make a (✓) below for each slide in which students are demonstrating appropriate fire drill procedures.

   _____ slide a   _____ slide b   _____ slide c

   _____ slide d   _____ slide e   _____ slide f

2. _____ *Objective*: The student will say the sounds of the letters b, d, and p, when each is shown.
   Assessment: I am going to show you a letter and make a letter sound. Raise your hand if the sound I make goes with the letter shown.
   a. Show p. . . . Say "puh."
   b. Show b. . . . Say "buh."
   c. Show d. . . . Say "duh."

3. _____ *Objective*: Given a list of *what*, *where*, or *when* reference questions, the student will write the name of an appropriate reference resource for answering each question.

   Assessment: What reference book would you use to answer the following questions?

   a. When was Abraham Lincoln born?

   Reference book: _____

   b. What is a synonym?

   Reference book: _____

   c. Where is the highest mountain in Africa?

   Reference book: _____

4. _____ *Objective*: Given descriptions of instances in which constitutional rights have been denied, the student will name the rights involved in each instance.

   Assessment: Name the constitutional rights guaranteed by the Bill of Rights.

PART 2. IDENTIFYING WELL-WRITTEN ASSESSMENT ITEMS

Mark an *X* by each item that is well written. Mark an *O* by each item that is not well written.

5. _____ Match the Spanish words with the English words that have the same meaning.

   _____ red   a. negro

   _____ blue   b. rojo

   _____ green   c. verde

   _____ black   d. azul

6. _____ If it is 10:35 now, what time will it be 40 minutes later?

7. _____ There are four classes of instruments in an orchestra. Name one and tell something about it.

8. _____ Prepare a topic outline for a persuasive speech on an issue of your choice.

PART 3. WRITING ASSESSMENT ITEMS

9. Write an item that would be appropriate for assessing student performance on the following instructional objective.
   Objective: Given a list of common foods, the student will name the food group (milk, meat, vegetable-fruit, bread-cereal) to which each belongs.
   Assessment:

10. Write an item for assessing student performance of the following objective.
    Objective: The student will voluntarily attend at least two theatrical events in the community during the semester.
    Assessment:

11. Write the directions to the student and criteria for assessing attainment of the following objective.
    Objective: The student will write a formal invitation for a given social event (such as a party, dance, or wedding).
    Directions:

    Criteria:

The answer key is on page 100.

ANSWER KEY

Part 1

1. *O* (inappropriate conditions and performance)
2. *O* (inappropriate performance)
3. *X*
4. *O* (inappropriate conditions)

Part 2

5. *O* (prompt—There are an equal number of items to be matched.)
6. *X*
7. *O* (clarity—What the description should include is not clear.)
8. *X*

Part 3

9. The assessment for this objective would include (1) giving the students a list of foods and (2) directing them to write or say the name of the food group to which each food belongs. A sample assessment item follows.
   Assessment: Write the food group to which each of the following foods belongs.
   a. *Cheese* _____
   b. *Oatmeal* _____
   c. *Carrots* _____
   d. *Hamburger* _____
   e. *Apple* _____
   Count your assessment item as correct if it is similar to the item just given. Your item should include a list of common foods, since that is specified as a given in the objective. It should not include the names of the food groups because the objective specifies that the student is to name the food group for each food.
10. The assessment item for this attitudinal objective could simply consist of directing the students to report their attendance at theatrical events during the semester. A sample item follows.
    Assessment: List the names of any plays, stage shows, or other theatrical events you attended this semester.
11. The assessment item for this objective would include (a) specifying a particular social event and (b) directing the students to prepare a formal invitation to the event. The criteria used to assess the

invitation the student prepares should include important characteristics of a well-written formal invitation. Following are sample
directions and criteria.

Directions: Write a formal invitation for a birthday dinner to be
given at your home.

Criteria: The invitation should be written in a formal style. It should
include the following information:

a. Time of the dinner (date and hour)
b. Place of the dinner
c. A request to confirm attendance (R.S.V.P.)

Score your item as correct if it contains directions and criteria
similar to those just given.

Now record your scores on the self test record form in Appendix A.

If you missed one or more items on any part of the self test, you may find
it helpful to reread the material related to that part of the test. Review of
the relevant section of the text is especially important if you missed a test
item and you do not understand why your answer was incorrect after
you have read the answers given above.

INDEX

104